Number 135
Fall 2012

New Directions for Evaluation

Sandra Mathison
Editor-in-Chief

Context: A Framework for Its Influence on Evaluation Practice

Debra J. Rog
Jody L. Fitzpatrick
Ross F. Conner
Editors

CONTEXT: A FRAMEWORK FOR ITS INFLUENCE ON EVALUATION PRACTICE
Debra J. Rog, Jody L. Fitzpatrick, Ross F. Conner (eds.)
New Directions for Evaluation, no. 135
Sandra Mathison, Editor-in-Chief

Microfilm copies of issues and articles are available in 16mm and 35mm, as well as microfiche in 105mm, through University Microfilms Inc., 300 North Zeeb Road, Ann Arbor, MI 48106-1346.

New Directions for Evaluation is indexed in Education Research Complete (EBSCO), ERIC Database (Education Resources Information Center), Higher Education Abstracts (Claremont Graduate University), SCOPUS (Elsevier), Social Services Abstracts (CSA/CIG), Sociological Abstracts (CSA/CIG), and Worldwide Political Science Abstracts (CSA/CIG).

NEW DIRECTIONS FOR EVALUATION (ISSN 1097-6736, electronic ISSN 1534-875X) is part of The Jossey-Bass Education Series and is published quarterly by Wiley Subscription Services, Inc., A Wiley Company, at Jossey-Bass, One Montgomery Street, Suite 1200, San Francisco, CA 94104-4594.

SUBSCRIPTIONS cost $89 for U.S./Canada/Mexico; $113 international. For institutions, agencies, and libraries, $295 U.S.; $335 Canada/Mexico; $369 international. Prices subject to change.

EDITORIAL CORRESPONDENCE should be addressed to the Editor-in-Chief, Sandra Mathison, University of British Columbia, 2125 Main Mall, Vancouver, BC V6T 1Z4, Canada.

www.josseybass.com

Editorial Policy and Procedures

New Directions for Evaluation, a quarterly sourcebook, is an official publication of the American Evaluation Association. The journal publishes empirical, methodological, and theoretical works on all aspects of evaluation. A reflective approach to evaluation is an essential strand to be woven through every issue. The editors encourage issues that have one of three foci: (1) craft issues that present approaches, methods, or techniques that can be applied in evaluation practice, such as the use of templates, case studies, or survey research; (2) professional issues that present topics of import for the field of evaluation, such as utilization of evaluation or locus of evaluation capacity; (3) societal issues that draw out the implications of intellectual, social, or cultural developments for the field of evaluation, such as the women's movement, communitarianism, or multiculturalism. A wide range of substantive domains is appropriate for *New Directions for Evaluation;* however, the domains must be of interest to a large audience within the field of evaluation. We encourage a diversity of perspectives and experiences within each issue, as well as creative bridges between evaluation and other sectors of our collective lives.

The editors do not consider or publish unsolicited single manuscripts. Each issue of the journal is devoted to a single topic, with contributions solicited, organized, reviewed, and edited by a guest editor. Issues may take any of several forms, such as a series of related chapters, a debate, or a long article followed by brief critical commentaries. In all cases, the proposals must follow a specific format, which can be obtained from the editor-in-chief. These proposals are sent to members of the editorial board and to relevant substantive experts for peer review. The process may result in acceptance, a recommendation to revise and resubmit, or rejection. However, the editors are committed to working constructively with potential guest editors to help them develop acceptable proposals.

Sandra Mathison, Editor-in-Chief
University of British Columbia
2125 Main Mall
Vancouver, BC V6T 1Z4
CANADA
e-mail: nde@eval.org

CONTENTS

approach. The authors explain the fundamental elements of IEF epistemology and offer several examples of IEF in evaluation in American Indian communities.

Editors' Notes

C ontext is a force in evaluation. It shapes our practice, influencing how we as evaluators approach and design our studies, how we carry them out, and how we report our findings. Context also moderates and mediates the outcomes of the programs and policies we evaluate.

The concept of context is not new to evaluation. In fact, in Chapter 1 of this issue, Fitzpatrick notes that over 900 citations to the word *context* result from a search of the *American Journal of Evaluation*. Theorists in the evaluation field have long recognized the role that context plays in shaping evaluations. Since the 1970s, Carol Weiss has written about the need to be sensitive to the political context (Weiss, 1972, 1973). Alkin (2004) clearly highlights the central role of context in his context-adapted utilization approach and offers the perspective that we use the various evaluation models available to us, but adapt them to the specific program context one is in. Patton, in both describing utilization focused evaluation (Patton, 1976, 2008) and more recently, in his work on developmental evaluation (Patton, 2011), highlights the effects of context on the work of the evaluator as well as on the programs, policies, and the people within them. In fact, he created developmental evaluation as an approach to use in dynamic program contexts.

What is new about context in this issue is focusing squarely on the role that it plays in practice and illuminating the specific features of context on our evaluation approach and on the effects and outcomes of programs. In addition, we propose both a context framework to order our thinking related to context and a technique, context assessment, to guide our actions in including systematically considerations of context in the conduct of evaluation. Based on the 2009 American Evaluation Association conference theme, context in evaluation, and incorporating several of the Presidential Strand contributions from that conference, this issue explores the ways in which attending to context may improve the quality of evaluation practice.

One of the impetuses for the focus on context is some of the recent discussion of the need for a productive dialogue on method choice (see Julnes & Rog, 2007). The debate over primacy of certain methods is often conducted without a more formal understanding and explication of context. The editors of this issue believe a more detailed and conscious understanding of context can help inform the dialogue. The goal would be to replace a method-first orientation where it still exists with one that puts context first.

The contributions span theory, methods, and practice in an effort to move to a more comprehensive conceptualization of context that can guide

New Directions for Evaluation, no. 135, Fall 2012 © Wiley Periodicals, Inc., and the American Evaluation Association. Published online in Wiley Online Library (wileyonlinelibrary.com) • DOI: 10.1002/ev.20023 our work. In Chapter 1, Jody L. Fitzpatrick provides an historical and theoretical foundation for the issue, introducing and defining what is meant by context. She reviews evaluators' treatment of context over the last 40 years, with an emphasis on the early evaluation theorists such as Stufflebeam, Stake, Weiss, Wholey, and Patton. She observes that what specific theorists choose to highlight is affected by the arenas in which they work (e.g., some federal, others local). Although the different writers highlight different elements of context that are important to our practice, there continues to be a lack of a unified theory or conceptualization of the potential elements in the context that influence our practice. In more current evaluation practices, Fitzpatrick notes that two areas that have informed our understanding of context are cross-cultural evaluation and international evaluation. Both sensitize us to different elements of culture that also may be relevant contextual factors in many evaluations. Understanding and having sensitivity to the role of cultural differences can help us in selecting measures, involving stakeholders, reporting results, and scaling and replicating the programs we study (Cram, 2012).

The remainder of the issue pivots off of the framework offered by Debra J. Rog in her presidential address and described more fully in Chapter 2, in which she describes the elements of context that evaluators should consider and illustrates the choices evaluators make to deal with these elements. In an effort to provide a more comprehensive analysis of context, Rog outlines five broad areas of context to consider in evaluation and the ways in which these areas and the dimensions within them shape our approaches to evaluation. In addition to understanding evaluation in context, Rog also describes how evaluators may increase the relevance and rigor of their studies by explicitly examining the role of context in evaluation. Rog encourages evaluators to place a similar amount of attention to studying the context as we have to studying and understanding implementation. Just as we have opened the black box of programs through an exploration of program theory and implementation, Rog suggests we navigate the "black hole of context" through approaches that explicitly identify and measure their influence.

Chapters 3–5 offer three very distinct examples and discussions of the role of context in evaluation. Chapter 3, by Linda P. Thurston and colleagues, highlights the problem of water quality improvement and illustrates the need for context sensitivity in evaluating interventions aimed at such a complex and ever-changing problem. The authors highlight how the problem and environment/setting areas of Rog's context framework, in particular, offer elements that are important to consider in choosing an evaluation approach.

The watershed approach to water quality described by Thurston and coworkers brings in issues of complexity related to governance and development of interventions. Because watersheds cross jurisdiction lines, there is not a single governing body, and stakeholders can include anyone who contributes to or depends on the water source or who can affect the quality of the water resources. In addition, efforts to control the negative impacts on water quality are typically voluntary approaches that encourage the use of best management practices. One of the challenges, for example, is understanding how to change the behavior of individuals and others who may live very far from the watershed and do not rely on it for recreation or a water source, but who can negatively affect the water quality (e.g., through their tilling practices). The challenge is exacerbated by the fact that the changes in behavior can take years before they make a measurable difference in the water quality. These challenges transfer into challenges for an evaluation, highlighting the need for a variety of stakeholders to be involved and consulted and the need to measure the social as well as environmental outcomes in assessing progress toward change. A compounding evaluation challenge, however, is the variability with which watershed stakeholders understand and accept social indicators as valid measures of change as well as the extent to which they value evaluation as a tool in decision making (what Thurston and colleagues refer to as "evaluation ethos").

In Chapter 4, Joan LaFrance and colleagues argue that context is central to evaluation and "culture infuses all contexts and defines methodology itself." They describe the indigenous evaluation framework (IEF) to illustrate a framework that is defined by context. They contend that indigenous evaluation does not just mean accommodating or attending to context but instead requires a fundamental shift in thinking about methodology and method. Indigenous ways of knowing provide the foundation of IEF and the methodology is informed by core values that honor place, community, gifts of each individual, and sovereignty. These values are defined at the tribal level and are understood through a "community's traditional knowledge, lived experience, and spiritual expressions." The authors describe the role of stories and metaphors as methods to obtain an understanding of lived experience, and they provide a number of examples of program metaphors. In the IEF, as the authors describe, "Evaluators step in rhythm with the community rather than setting their own pace." Context defines everything in IEF; as they note in the title, context writes the script of an evaluation. In their perspective, therefore, IEF goes beyond the framework Rog posits to note that context does not just sit alongside relevance and rigor, but defines them and also defines what counts as actionable evidence. Context is the central element in indigenous evaluation.

Peter Dahler-Larsen and Thomas A. Schwandt also see context as central, but take issue with an approach such as Rog's that attempts to codify and inventory the types of context and their respective dimensions. The authors contend, as illustrated by two accounts of Danish culture, that context and evaluation practices are coconstructed. How evaluators make sense of a particular context is not independent of how the context structures the understanding for the evaluator. The level of involvement an evaluator has with an evaluand affects how an evaluator understands the context and gives the evaluator access to certain kinds of evidence. The context also shapes the evaluation processes. The authors do not believe a rational process of trying to scope a context is wise or fruitful. Because of the dynamic process of construction and reconstruction of context that occurs and the fact that theories and approaches are already interpretations of the context and the experiences the evaluators have made, the evaluators cannot observe the context as if they were detached from it. Even if an inventory were possible, there is no guarantee that it would lead to a clear choice. Overall, therefore, the authors note that their view of context, especially with respect to political culture, is more complex, indeterminable, and less easily accounted for than is communicated by frameworks that specify the elements and areas.

Chapters 3–5, together with the historical overview by Fitzpatrick and the framework by Rog, highlight several themes.

- The importance of culture within any conceptualization of context. Rog's framework identifies the importance of culture, but does not address it to the depth offered by the other contributors. Each of these builds upon and extends in important ways how culture is a central dimension to context.
- The level of involvement with an evaluand affects an evaluator's understanding of context, and the nature of that involvement shapes the type of access he or she may have to the information for the evaluations. This point was underscored by Dahler-Larsen and Schwandt, who noted that where evaluators are located, who they work for, and the types of data accessed all have a bearing on how they construct context. LaFrance and colleagues speak of the importance of working deeply with indigenous cultures and communities. Thurston and colleagues do not explicitly note the evaluator's level of involvement, but do imply a certain level of involvement in order to establish stakeholder buy-in for evaluation, to collaborate to develop a systematic cultural change within the community to adopt an evaluation ethos, and to build the evaluation capacity of the local stakeholders. In addition, although Rog does not discuss the evaluator's level of involvement in the evaluation in relation to gaining knowledge, the level of involvement is implied by her emphasis of working closely with stakeholders, especially consumers and beneficiaries of the evaluand, in gaining an understanding of context. The point implicitly made by Rog is that the very distance that is often built into federal evaluations necessitates that the evaluator try to gain more context sensitivity, not in a checklist fashion, but in a manner that thinks through the variety of areas and dimensions that are important to consider in scoping the effort.

- Context affects the choice of evaluation approach. The history of evaluation has demonstrated that the discipline of the evaluator and stakeholders influence, appropriately or inappropriately, the approach selected. Dahler-Larsen and Schwandt contend, however, that although not all approaches are equally appropriate in all contexts, they do not believe the solution is a "matching scheme" between a particular set of contextual factors and a particular approach. They note that different approaches already are based on interpretations of the context. The point made by Rog, and illustrated by Thurston and colleagues and LaFrance and colleagues, is that greater context sensitivity does not lead to a paint-by-numbers approach to evaluation design, but rather, increases the probability that the design, methods, and overall approach will be more appropriate to the conditions at the time, will incorporate a broader range of perspectives, and will likely be more successful (i.e., able to be carried out).

In Chapter 6 of this issue, the editors of the issue (led by Ross F. Conner) revisit the context framework, informed by the three cases that have been presented and the new aspects that have been raised, and describe a process we label *context assessment* (CA) that provides a means of integrating context and its implications within the important stages of evaluation. Although we recognize the limitations of such an approach and heed the Dahler-Larsen and Schwandt cautions of any such process leading to a simplistic and ill-advised inventorying of all contextual elements, we see the type of CA process we propose as ultimately having benefits for all involved in an evaluation. We believe that such a process will provide the evaluator with an opportunity to anchor and then reanchor the evaluation with explicit attention to different context issues and that it will make formal, and thus more salient, what are often issues that are fleetingly and informally considered. We do not expect that CA will guarantee the identification of all relevant factors, and we recognize that this approach will be filtered through the evaluator's perspectives, experiences, and background. We are aware that adding an explicit CA process will add to the time and budget of an evaluation, but we believe this addition may be money and time that can add to the richness of the evaluation process.

If context matters, as Rog stated at the outset of her presidential address and in Chapter 2 of this issue, the context framework gives us a way to organize our discussions and context assessment provides a way to act on it. We believe our experiences and those of others, such as the authors in this issue, have demonstrated the utility of paying attention to context in an explicit way. The context framework and the CA process provide a way to do this systematically so that we can begin to deepen and share our knowledge of how contextual factors operate in all stages of evaluation.

NEW DIRECTIONS FOR EVALUATION • DOI: 10.1002/ev

References

Alkin, M. (2004). Context adapted utilization: A personal journey. In M. Alkin (Ed.), *Evaluation roots: Tracing theorists' views and influences.* Thousand Oaks, CA: Sage.

Cram, F. (2012, February 12). Remarks on American Evaluation's "Thought Leaders Forum."

Julnes, G., & Rog, D. J. (Eds.). (2007). Informing federal policies on evaluation methodology: Building the evidence base for method choice in government sponsored evaluations. *New Directions for Evaluation, 113.*

Patton, M. Q. (1976). *Utilization-focused evaluation.* Beverly Hills, CA: Sage.

Patton, M. Q. (2008). *Utilization-focused evaluation* (4th ed.). Thousand Oaks, CA: Sage.

Patton, M. Q. (2011). *Developmental evaluation: Appling complexity concepts to enhance innovation and use.* New York, NY: Guilford Press.

Weiss, C. H. (1972). *Evaluation research: Methods for assessing program effectiveness.* Englewood Cliffs, NJ: Prentice-Hall.

Weiss, C. H. (1973). Where politics and evaluation research meet. *Evaluation,* 37–45.

Wholey, J. S. (1979). *Evaluation: Promise and performance.* Washington, DC: The Urban Institute.

Debra J. Rog
Jody L. Fitzpatrick
Ross F. Conner
Editors

DEBRA J. ROG *is an associate director at Westat and president of The Rockville Institute. She was the 2009 president of the American Evaluation Association.*

JODY L. FITZPATRICK *is associate professor in the School of Public Affairs at the University of Colorado, Denver, and will be the president of the American Evaluation Association in 2013.*

ROSS F. CONNER *is professor emeritus at the University of California– Ivine, in the School of Social Ecology, Department of Planning, Policy and Design, and is a past president of the American Evaluation Association and of the International Organization for Cooperation in Evaluation (IOCE).*

NEW DIRECTIONS FOR EVALUATION • DOI: 10.1002/ev

Fitzpatrick, J. L. (2012). An introduction to context and its role in evaluation practice. In
D. J. Rog, J. L. Fitzpatrick, & R. F. Conner (Eds.), *Context: A framework for its influence
on evaluation practice. New Directions for Evaluation, 135,* 7–24.

1

An Introduction to Context and Its Role in Evaluation Practice

Jody L. Fitzpatrick

Abstract

*Evaluators have written about the need to consider context in conducting eval-
uations, but most such admonitions are broad. Context is not developed fully.
This chapter reviews the evaluation literature on context and discusses the two
areas in which context has been more carefully considered by evaluators: the culture of program participants when their culture is different from the predominant one and the cultural norms of program participants in countries outside
the West. We have learned much about how the culture of participants or communities can affect evaluation and should continue our learning there. Evaluators also need to expand their consideration of context to consider the program
itself and its setting and the political norms of audiences, decision makers, and
other stakeholders of the program.* © Wiley Periodicals, Inc., and the American Evaluation Association.

Context. What do we mean by context? Consider the context in which
you are reading this chapter. First, of course, there is the setting—the
room and building in which you are reading. But the context for reading this chapter also includes your own background, knowledge, and beliefs
about evaluation and its role in society; about governments; about clients,
communities, and programs. Context is an amorphous issue. Many evaluators have written of the importance of context to evaluation practice. This

chapter summarizes some of the relevant literature to acquaint the reader with different approaches to context in evaluation and the factors to consider in conceptualizing context.

The importance of context to evaluation has been cited by authors since the beginnings of program evaluation in the United States (Stake, 1974; Stufflebeam, 1971; Weiss, 1972). A search of the *American Journal of Evaluation* reveals 902 citations for the word *context*. The *Program Evaluation Standards* (Joint Committee on Standards for Educational Evaluation, 2011) and Guiding Principles for Evaluators [American Evaluation Association (AEA), 2004] both refer to the importance of considering context in conducting evaluations. The *Sage Handbook of Evaluation* (Shaw, Greene, & Mark, 2005) includes three chapters concerning different contextual issues in evaluation. Finally, the "Evaluation Roadmap for a More Effective Government," developed by the AEA Evaluation Policy Task Force (2009) to guide evaluation policy and management at the federal level, emphasizes context. They note that one evaluation strategy or design does not meet the needs of all programs nor all stakeholders or decision makers. Evaluations must be adapted to the history and stage of the program and be conducted in a manner that "is appropriate for program stewardship and useful for decision making" (p. 3).

Yet the various contextual factors that influence evaluation are rarely considered in much depth in the evaluation literature. Nods and admonitions are given to the importance of considering context and to its impact on evaluation plans, methods, implementation, and use, but few develop the construct in depth. Many evaluators focus on particular aspects of context that are particularly relevant to their own experience and approach to evaluation (Greene, 2005). But Greene notes there is a need for "a more sophisticated conceptualization and study of just how context matters in evaluation" (p. 84). We hope to begin a dialogue that will bring about more sophisticated conceptualizations of context to spark evaluators to consider and study how context matters. The different facets of context brought together here teach us something about what we mean by context and the factors we should consider in planning and conducting an evaluation, and illustrate where we still need to go in defining and elaborating on context.

Let us begin by considering some definitions of context. The *Oxford English Language Dictionary* (Oxford University Press, 2010) defines context as "the circumstances that form the setting for an event, statement, or idea, and in terms of which it can be fully understood or assessed." The first part of the definition uses the broad term *circumstances* to refer to the myriad factors that comprise context; the latter part of the definition, however, is particularly noteworthy for evaluation. This part of the definition stresses its purpose; that is, knowledge of context is necessary in order to fully understand or assess something. The dictionary further defines the common phrase *out of context* as meaning "without the surrounding words or circumstances and so not fully understandable" (Oxford University Press,

2010). Thus, in settings broader than evaluation knowledge of context refers to the purpose of understanding something fully.

More specific to the field of evaluation, Greene (2005) defines context as "the setting within which the evaluand (the program, policy, or product being evaluated) and thus the evaluation are situated. Context is the site, location, environment, or milieu for a given evaluand" (p. 83). She identifies five specific dimensions to context in evaluation: demographic characteristics of the setting and the people in it, material and economic features, institutional and organizational climate, interpersonal dimensions or typical means of interaction and norms for relationships in the setting, and political dynamics of the setting, including issues and interests. Her identification of five dimensions of the contexts of evaluations is an important contribution to our beginning to think about context in a comprehensive, systematic fashion.

Others write about context with a focus on cultural contexts and the practice of evaluation that is responsive to different cultures, often ethnic or racial communities with less political power whose values have been ignored (Chouinard & Cousins, 2009; Frierson, Hood, & Hughes, 2002; SenGupta, Hopson, & Thompson-Robinson, 2004). In these writings, although the term *culture* is predominant, the terms *context* and *culture* are often used interchangeably. See, for example, Prado's (2011) article entitled "'Honor the Context': Opening Lines for a Critical Multicultural Evaluative Practice." Thomas (2004), however, differentiates culture and context. In describing a contextually-responsive evaluation framework and its use in urban schools in the United States, she sees context as broader than culture and defines context as

> the combination of factors (including culture) accompanying the implementation and evaluation of a project that might influence its results, including geographical location, timing, political and social climate, economic conditions, and other things going on at the same time as the project. It includes the totality of the environment in which the project takes place. (p. 11)

Chouinard and Cousins (2009) also define context as subsuming culture, noting that context is "the site of confluence where program, culture, and community connect" (p. 461).

Historical Roots of Context in Evaluation

Evaluators writing in the early years of the field in the United States, the 1970s and into the 1980s, began to indirectly, and sometimes directly, define context for us. With a focus on use, though at different levels, they tended to focus on the context of those making the decisions. Stufflebeam's new model moved evaluators from automatically concluding that their purpose was to determine whether objectives had been achieved to thinking about what decisions the managers were facing and how evaluation information might help them in making those decisions (Stufflebeam, 1968). (Unfortunately, today we seem to be moving back to automatically evaluating the achievement of objectives, today called *outcomes*, with a focus on accountability rather than use.) His development of the context–input–process–product (CIPP) evaluation model, is one of the early uses of the word *context* in evaluation (Stufflebeam, 1968, 1971). But Stufflebeam's stages of evaluation were concerned with the stage of the program and the type of evaluation that might be appropriate. A context evaluation was conducted at the early stages of a program and its primary focus was needs assessment. Thus, the CIPP evaluation Web site indicates that context evaluation "assesses needs, assets, and problems within a defined environment" and is intended to answer the question "What needs to be done?" (http://www.wmich.edu/evalctr/archive_checklists/cippchecklist, 2007, p. 4). One element of the CIPP Evaluation Model Checklist (Stufflebeam, 2007) encourages the evaluator to "monitor and record data on the program's environment, including related programs, area resources, area needs and problems, and political dynamics," but the other elements of a context evaluation are concerned with assessing and determining the needs of program recipients to provide users with information on how to plan the intended program. Nevertheless, Stufflebeam brought evaluators' attention in these early years to management and decision makers. As such, he awakened evaluators' concern about Rog's decision-making context (Rog, 2012). The evaluator was to learn about managers, their decisions, and the organizational context in which they were made in order to provide useful information.

Stake's responsive model (1974) also dealt with context, but his focus was more on the program deliverers, in his case, teachers. The responsive model was developed in reaction to the dominant preordinate approach of the time, large studies designed to test big theories with fixed, quantitative methods. Greene and Abma (2001, p. 1) note that Stake reframed evaluation "from the application of sophisticated analytic techniques that address distant policymakers' questions on program benefits and effectiveness 'on the average,' to an engagement with on-site practitioners about the quality and meanings of their practice." Thus, Stake was calling upon evaluators to be responsive and, among other things, to focus on the local—local knowledge, local theories, and the events of an individual program. Like Stufflebeam, he wanted to shift evaluators from a focus entirely on objectives, but his solution was to become closer to the program, observing it, talking with program deliverers and drawing out their thoughts and perceptions, and developing case studies or in-depth descriptions of the program. Stake was moving evaluators toward seeing the program and, in so doing, to understand the program's context. Thus, Stake (1980, p. 76) writes, "An evaluation will probably not be useful if the evaluator does not know the interests or the language of his audiences." He recognized that stakeholders held different values and that it was important for the evaluator to bring out their different value perspectives. By learning the interests, language, and values of audiences in a program, generally teachers and administrators, evaluators following Stake's model consequently would become aware of different issues in the program's context, not just information needs or decisions. But, primarily, Stake wanted to give voice to local users, to build on their expert knowledge, and to increase their control over their program (Stake, 1980) so that it could be responsive to local needs. He fought the uniformity he felt the federal government and outside experts were imposing on schools. Stake believed that local settings, local characteristics, and context make a difference in education.

Stufflebeam and Stake both worked in educational settings and, as such, these contexts affected their approaches to evaluation. As Stake's beliefs demonstrate, schools in the United States were, and in most cases still are, primarily local institutions intended to respond to local needs. Although federal funds had prompted the growth of educational evaluation, the focus was still local. Meanwhile, other early evaluators (Weiss, Datta, Wholey) were working for the federal government conducting evaluations on a variety of large, often costly, social programs. The evaluations they conducted were often the ones referred to by Greene and Abma when they cite evaluations applying "sophisticated analytic techniques that address distant policy-makers' questions on program benefits 'on the average.'" Their potential audiences included elected officials and political appointees who had the power to make decisions regarding continuation, expansion, or elimination of national programs or their pilots. Influenced by this context, Carol Weiss became disappointed with policy makers' failure to make much use of program evaluation (Weiss, 1972, 1973.) Her chapter on "The Turbulent Setting of the Action Program" in her early and influential evaluation text (Weiss, 1972) described sources of friction between evaluators and program planners, including differences in goals, roles, values, interests, and frames of reference. Weiss provides more detail than previous writers on how these two groups differ. Her goal was to make evaluators aware of the strikingly different contexts of program planners and, in turn, help evaluators increase the use of their studies. She also addressed the importance of other contexts including the social context of the program, its setting, and the "social frameworks of neighborhood and community" and "national systems of values, laws, and sensitivities," noting that "local mores even determine what can be studied and what cannot" (Weiss, 1972, p. 108). And, foreshadowing today's discussions on culturally responsive evaluation, Weiss discussed the need for evaluators to explore the social context of program participants writing "He [the program participant] does not come to the program empty, unattached, or unanchored. He has beliefs and values, he has friends and relatives, habits, patterns of behavior, and ideas. . . . One implication for evaluation may be the value of exploring the supportive and inhibiting features of the interpersonal context. It might investigate the attitudes and behaviors of key people in the participant's environment (family, coworkers, teachers)" (Weiss, 1972, p. 108). She encourages evaluators to become aware of these many contextual factors, closing with "The lesson for the evaluator is: Be alert. The studies that are ultimately most practical and useful are often those that open our eyes to new elements on the scene" (Weiss, 1972, p. 109). Thus, Weiss made early evaluators aware of the importance of studying additional contextual elements in an effort to increase the use and impact of evaluations.

Wholey, also working with evaluation in the U.S. federal government, shared Weiss's concerns about use (Wholey, 1979, 1987). To learn more about the problem, Wholey and his colleagues studied federal evaluations and identified three apparent causes for the failure of evaluations to be used and to improve programs: lack of definition, lack of clear logic, and lack of management (Horst, Nay, Scanlon, & Wholey, 1974). Wholey developed evaluability assessment to counter these problems. Today, we recall evaluability assessment primarily for its contribution of the use of logic models to help in defining the problem, establishing goals, and linking program actions to those goals. But evaluability assessments also required the evaluator to attend to some new critical contextual issues for the program and the evaluation: the managers and their ability and motivation to use evaluations to improve programs. Wholey's attention to managers and the decision context in which they operated was a new step in examining context.

Michael Patton's original utilization-focused model (Patton, 1976) followed Wholey's focus on managers and encouraged use by identifying one key manager who has the position to do something with the evaluation and the disposition, or interest, to use it. Patton's model moved evaluators to begin thinking more about the organizational contexts in which their evaluations were used and to explore those contexts in thinking about utility. He made different and more specific suggestions for evaluators to use in working with managers.

All these early evaluators, Stufflebeam, Stake, Weiss, Wholey, and Patton, were encouraging evaluators to become more familiar with the context of the program and the managers and deliverers who were responsible for it. Weiss added more in noting the importance of contextual factors for participants and, more broadly, contextual elements of the community, state, or country. However, the arenas in which these evaluators worked differed, and these different arenas explained some of their different emphases concerning context. Wholey and Weiss evaluated federal programs, and their audiences were federal policy makers. As such, they were more distant from the programs they evaluated and considered political contexts in more depth. Stufflebeam, Stake, and Patton were working more closely with individual programs or schools, and thus could attend to the specific contextual circumstances of a school or a program setting.

More recently, Pawson and Tilley (1997) have proposed a model of realistic evaluation that makes explicit use of context in a quite different way. Rather than considering contextual elements to increase use or to give voice to local issues, their purpose is to use context to explain different program effects. They note that few programs fail completely or work perfectly. Instead, most programs succeed in some contexts with some clients. The evaluator's job, then, is to identify those contextual elements that prompt a program to succeed or fail. Pawson and Tilley propose developing context–mechanism–outcome configurations to describe and explain program success.

The above are models of evaluation that their authors hope will influence evaluators in their practice. Some models require more allegiance, and less deviation, than others. More recent research on evaluators' actual practice shows that evaluators do not follow one model (Christie, 2003), but adapt, though the results on why they are adapting are not quite clear. Fitzpatrick's interviews of well-known evaluators shows that they do adapt to a variety of contextual elements, including the culture of the participants, what is known in the field of the program, views and interests of citizens and other stakeholders, the stage of the program, and the culture of the organization (Fitzpatrick, Christie, & Mark, 2009). These interviews highlight some of the different contextual elements that cause experienced evaluators to adapt and change their practices; yet they, too, fail to lead us to a comprehensive view of the potential contextual elements that might affect an evaluation.

Today, many evaluation models and approaches call for working closely with managers, program deliverers, and clients to learn more about their preferences and interests in both the program and in the evaluation, their values, and for clients and community, their culture. As such, most evaluators have moved from an early experimental, "hands off" tradition where they were concerned that their involvement might change the program or threaten the perceived neutrality of the evaluation to one in which evaluators are immersed in the program. These activities give evaluators the potential to consider and learn about context, but being immersed does not mean one notices the water. To illustrate the merits of considering context and its effect on evaluation more carefully, we review two particular areas of evaluation that have taught us more about context and its importance: cross-cultural or multicultural evaluation and international evaluations.

Cross-Cultural Evaluation: Culture as Context

As the United States has grown increasingly diverse in race and ethnicity, and as educational and social programs often serve people from minority or disadvantaged groups, evaluators have begun to realize that we need to know more about the context and culture of the clients served by the programs we are evaluating. In the 1940s and 1950s, two African American educational evaluators, Aaron Brown and Leander Boykin, made others aware of the special needs and history of African Americans and argued that evaluators should seek their perspectives in conducting evaluations (Hood, 2001). Almost 40 years later, in her presidential address to members of the American Evaluation Association, Kirkhart (1995, p. 1) urged evaluators to turn their attention to culture, stating "multicultural influences shape and are shaped by our work."

Since then, many have written about multicultural evaluation (Conner, 2005), cross-cultural evaluation (Chouinard & Cousins, 2009), and cultural competence (Thompson-Robinson, Hopson, & SenGupta, 2004). Frierson, Hood, and Hughes (2002) developed a model for culturally responsive evaluation (CRE) and have since expanded on the model (Hood, Hopson, & Frierson, 2005; Hopson, 2009). By 2009, the practice of cross-cultural evaluation had spread such that Chouinard and Cousins (2009) identified 52 evaluations making use of cross-cultural principles and used these articles to examine trends and propose a theoretical framework for future research. These writings help evaluators recognize their responsibilities to attend to cultures different from their own or different from the dominant culture, seek knowledge and understanding of different cultures, and involve stakeholders from participating cultures in the planning, conduct, interpretation, and reporting of the evaluation. U.S. evaluators, who are primarily from white, middle-class, educated backgrounds, have recognized that their own personal contexts and values influence how they see, or fail to see, other cultures. As such, our evaluations are invalid. They become invalid in many ways: by identifying the wrong questions to frame the evaluation, by ignoring key stakeholders who are potentially strong users of the evaluation, by misinterpreting stakeholders' priorities or even program goals, by collecting data with the use of words or nonverbal cues that have different meanings to the audience, by failing to describe the program accurately or to understand its outcomes because the evaluator is unable to notice nuances or subtleties of the culture, by reporting results in means only accessible by the dominant culture or those in positions of power, and so on.

Understanding different cultures is not an easy task. Stafford Hood, one of the developers of culturally-responsive evaluation, has written, "It is difficult, if not impossible for evaluators to see, hear, and understand cultural nuances that differ from their lived experience" (2005, p. 97). He and others have proposed practical, specific methods for beginning to understand those cultures. These methods include careful examination of one's own values, assumptions, and cultural context; inclusion of community members and program participants in evaluation planning and other phases; careful observation and respectful interactions and reflection on what has been learned; and training the evaluation team to be culturally responsive (Frierson et al., 2002; Madison, 2007; SenGupta et al., 2004). Most recently,

McBride (2011) has used sociocultural theory to suggest new strategies for conducting culturally responsive evaluations, including collecting data on local history from existing documents and through interviews with local leaders.

Most pertinent to this chapter is what this literature has taught us about the dimension of context that concerns culture. The writings on culture in evaluation typically focus on racial or ethnic cultures in the United States, although evaluators in New Zealand have also written about their work with indigenous New Zealanders and the need to gain cultural competence (Cram, 2012; Cram, Smith, & Johnstone, 2003). Generally, the cultures discussed are those of groups of individuals, for example, African Americans, American Indians, or Māori in New Zealand, and are considered because they are typically program recipients. These authors have alerted us to elements of context that we have not previously considered carefully: the norms and history of racial or ethnic groups in a particular community, school, or geographic area; their verbal and nonverbal means of communication; their norms concerning interpersonal interactions and dealing with people from other classes and cultures (like the evaluator); and, finally, their values and beliefs regarding the program, the needs it is addressing, its outcomes and activities, the evaluation, and the evaluation team and individuals on it. We must consider these cultural differences in selecting measures, in involving stakeholders, in reporting results, and in considering scalability and transferability of a program or policy to another setting (Cram, 2012). From this literature, evaluators learn that we cannot list all the elements of culture any more than we can totally know a culture. But, as with our initial discussions of context, we can learn to learn more, to observe, to listen, and to be aware of these dimensions in order to conduct better evaluations.

One observation from this literature on culture and its role in evaluation: The authors tend to be from the educational evaluation arena. Their organizational context is schools. The cultural diversity in U.S. schools today and the increasing pressure on schools to close the achievement gap and to help all students achieve high educational standards may have made these evaluators more sensitive than those in other fields to the importance of learning more about the racial and ethnic culture of students. But other elements of context have also influenced educational evaluators to attend to culture. Schools are local, identifiable, and valued by the community, generally well known by many who live there and considered important to the community's quality of life. Schools may bring together groups who are often apart and who have different cultures and values, different student and parent groups, teachers, school administrators, and coaches. Their work in schools has raised the awareness of evaluators in other arenas—social services, community development, employment, the environment—to the need to consider the culture of those served by the program. Finally, culturally responsive evaluations have been primarily a U.S. phenomenon, perhaps because the United States is more diverse than many countries. The large majority (79%) of the cross-cultural studies found by Chouinard and Cousins (2009) were conducted in the United States and the most common organizational contexts were education and health.

Cross-cultural evaluation models and practice have increased our awareness of contextual issues pertinent to the culture of clients and community stakeholders, especially those from minority racial and ethnic groups, but much of the writing is primarily concerned with the context of the United States and schools. Will these issues and needs continue to emerge in other policy settings, in other countries, and with other racial and ethnic cultures? Certainly so, but we need to develop more knowledge of cultural norms that may affect programs and evaluations, power and dialogue, and ultimately understanding. We also need to be aware that cultural competence is needed in every evaluation, not just those where the cultural norms "hit us in the face" as being different from our own. Every group of participants has, or develops, a culture and that culture influences the program and the evaluation. (Consider, for example, a cohort of students completing a program together. Each develops its own somewhat different culture that is important for the program administrators, instructors, and evaluators to consider.)

Contextual Factors Arising From Literature on International Evaluations

Examinations of the practice of evaluation in different countries have made evaluators aware of other important contextual factors, in particular the influence of governments, public administration, and citizens' and policy makers' expectations for evaluation. Recognizing how international evaluations have informed us, Michael Patton, in an interview with King and Greenseid (Patton, King, & Greenseid, 2007, p. 12) observed "international diversity [in evaluation practice] is challenging our thinking about what constitutes good evaluation work and what it means for evaluation to be used in different cultural and political contexts." Nevo first called evaluators' attention to contextual differences across countries in his 1982 article on international evaluation. Nevo, an educational evaluator in Israel, was concerned that American models of evaluation were not likely to be valid in other countries. He noted that the United States is a democratic country where citizens' "right to know" prompted the start of evaluation and influenced evaluation practices and models. Today in the United States, there is widespread distrust of government. These elements of the political context influence evaluation choices and approaches. And, these contextual elements differ across countries.

Almost 30 years after the publication of Nevo's article, evaluation has grown rapidly in other countries, but the nature of evaluation in those countries differs dramatically (Fitzpatrick, Sanders, & Worthen, 2011; Rist, 1990; Stern, 2005). A study by Rist and his colleagues (Rist, 1990) of eight Western countries found historic governmental policies influenced the nature of present-day evaluation in those countries. First-wave countries, so called because evaluation started earlier in these countries, began evaluation with an emphasis on social experimentation and program improvement, for example, the United States and the Great Society in the 1960s. In these countries, evaluation was often decentralized, with evaluators working closely with the programs they were evaluating, reporting to them on how to improve. Second-wave countries, including the United Kingdom countries, the Netherlands, Denmark, and France, began evaluation during the 1980s, during the Margaret Thatcher era. There, evaluation was intended to help control national budgets and reduce government spending. Evaluation in these countries was typically centralized, reporting to high-level government agencies and officials concerned with summative decisions about programs and budgets. Although concern with accountability has become a norm today in many first-wave countries, early traditions remain. In the United States, evaluations are often conducted by independent consultants. Internal evaluations are sometimes viewed with suspicion (Love, 1991). And most evaluations concern educational or social programs. As such, American evaluators are more likely to have been educated in psychology or education with a focus on individuals as the units of analysis than European evaluators (http://www.eval.org/Scan/aea08.scan .report.pdf). (The AEA environmental scan referenced here is of AEA members. Many evaluators who conduct evaluation work in the United States are not members of AEA and have backgrounds in other areas.) In Europe, evaluators are more likely to be schooled in economics and political science than American evaluators. They study programs ranging from agriculture to transportation; having arisen from a concern over government spending, evaluations focus on many different issues (Fitzpatrick, Sanders, & Worthen, 2011). By examining differences in evaluation across countries, we become aware of the influence that government policies and directions have on evaluation. These policies and views about evaluation and its role are critical elements of the context of evaluation.

Stern (2005) identifies many "contextual challenges" for evaluation today, drawing on his experience as a practitioner in Europe and the United Kingdom and as president of their respective evaluation societies. Like many evaluators outside the United States, he sees political issues at the national and international level as central to the context of evaluation. Some of these contextual challenges, he writes, are "driven by global shifts in the nature of the State and public policy that are reshaping evaluation practice" (Stern, 2005, p. 293). New public management, decentralization and privatization of some government services, and greater attention to transparency and accountability have influenced evaluation in many Western countries. Stern observes that evaluators in Europe are more concerned with policy, and decision makers expect evaluators to have knowledge of policy content. In fact, Fitzpatrick observed that evaluators in France and Spain generally use the term *policy evaluation* rather than *program evaluation* and there was an intended, meaningful difference. Policies are generally broader than programs, and thus the object of the evaluation differs. Stern (2005, p. 299) concurs, noting that European policy makers believe that "piecemeal evaluation of individual programmes are not simply additive; many good programmes do not make a good policy." Again, we see government having an important influence on the nature of our work, influencing the nature and scope of what is evaluated.

But geography and culture influence evaluation differently in other countries as well. Dahler-Larsen and Schwandt, in this issue, describe how elements of the Danish political culture affect what is evaluated and the questions that are asked (Dahler-Larsen & Schwandt, 2012). For example, the European Union and OECD publish many comparisons of European countries. The comparisons have a growing influence on Danish citizens' and policymakers' views of Denmark and policy priorities. In contrast, the United States is not part of a multi-country organization like the EU. Further, its size and geographical isolation from other countries leads to a reliance on comparisons among the 50 states, rather than across countries. Americans and Danes also differ in their views of the roles and responsibilities of government. Many Americans want to minimize the role of government and distrust its actions and intents. These views lead evaluation to focus on accountability, outcomes, and the achievement of standards (Fitzpatrick et al., 2011). In contrast, Danish citizens are more trusting of their government and see government as playing an important role in income redistribution and maintaining the welfare of citizens (Dahler-Larsen & Schwandt, 2012).

But, our review so far has concerned only political contexts in Western countries. The context for evaluation in developing countries is quite different and varied. In many of these countries, evaluation was introduced by multinational development agencies like the World Bank and UN organizations. Nongovernmental organizations (NGOs) like World Vision, OXFAM, and CARE also play major roles in funding and conducting evaluations in such countries (Bamberger, 1999). Capacity building is a major focus in some countries (http://afrea.org/home/index.cfm). But the political and cultural context for evaluation in these countries is quite different. Bhola (2003) notes that evaluation is sometimes viewed as a Western notion imposed by former colonial powers.

In many of those countries, citizens' relationships and their concerns with government differ sharply from those in the West. Bamberger (1999) observes that evaluators who seek participation from local stakeholders or collect data in ways that conflict with community norms may unknowingly create problems, loss of services, rejection, or violence for those who participate. Both cultural norms and nondemocratic governments can provoke these challenges and others. Men may object to their wives or children participating in data collection, such as interviews outside of their presence. Village leaders may perceive the evaluation, participatory efforts, or data collection as threatening their authority. Government officials may limit services of those believed to be critical of government actions and restrict the choices and actions of the evaluator or dissemination of information.

Perhaps because the context of these evaluations is so different, evaluators are more likely to recognize the importance of learning about local contexts and cultural norms than when they are working in their own country. Stevenson and Thomas (2005, p. 215) state that "external evaluators [in developing countries] cannot design effective evaluations without incorporating 'local knowledge.'" This need to incorporate local knowledge and to be observant of different political and social customs and expectations is a central focus of such evaluations. In contrast, culturally responsive evaluation has had to awaken American evaluators to the need to become culturally competent. In the context of public health evaluations in developing countries, Stevenson and Thomas see the environment contributing to "the development of a pragmatic, culture-sensitized approach to evaluation traditions" (2005, p. 218). Paradigm wars as seen in the United States in the 1990s have not occurred in developing countries; instead, these evaluators are comfortable with a wide range of qualitative and quantitative methods. Evaluations measuring cost effectiveness is more often a major focus of evaluation in these countries with scarce resources. In Africa, evaluations of development projects and consideration of human rights and gender issues are major topics for the African Evaluation Association (http://afrea.org). Again, we see the context of the country—the nature of government and its policies, expectations of NGOs and multinational development agencies, cultural norms of individuals and communities—all issues beyond the specific program to be evaluated, affecting the nature of the evaluation, the questions to be addressed, the methods of data collection, and stakeholder participation.

International evaluations also make us aware of widely different cultural norms—norms concerning communication, consensus, and conflict, openness to new information, styles of decision making—and their effects on evaluation practice. Nevo (1982) identifies these and other related issues as a major factor in considering the validity of American evaluation models in other countries:

> Without discussing the validity of such concepts as national character or national personality, one might suspect some differences in personal characteristics among decision-makers and evaluators in various societies. Rationality, punctuality, intellectual curiosity, need for structure or tolerance for ambiguity might be of special relevance to the conduct of evaluation. (p. 74)

NEW DIRECTIONS FOR EVALUATION • DOI: 10.1002/ev

Examples of such differences and their effects on evaluation have emerged since in discussions of evaluation in different countries. Patton (2007) cites cultural differences between Japan and the United States that have strong implications for the communication of evaluation information. He comments that he has found "perspectives for handling feedback and engaging in learning to be fundamentally different in Asian contexts" (p.112), observing that Americans tend to have a "very competitive and blaming culture." As such, pointing out problems with or failures in individual programs is more or less expected in American evaluations. In contrast, in Japan social harmony is a much stronger cultural value and "for the sake of group harmony, they're not into blaming and embarrassing people and pointing out their faults" (Patton et al., 2007, p. 112). Thus, communicating results of an evaluation in these different cultural contexts must be handled in a quite different way. Fitzpatrick's American norms for communication created difficulties in Spain. Communication that would be seen as forthright and constructive, albeit negative, in the United States was avoided in Spain and, as such, obtaining input or reactions from stakeholders and colleagues was more difficult and took much more time.

Every country has different cultural and political norms that affect many aspects of evaluation from selection of evaluation questions, stakeholders and potential users, methods of data collection, and means for reporting. Evaluators who work in countries different from their own recognize the need to include evaluators native to that country on their evaluation team and to be sensitive to the quite different context in which their evaluation is conducted. Wallis, Dukay, and Fitzpatrick (2008) describe how they worked with a multidisciplinary evaluation team composed of evaluators from the United States and from Tanzania to evaluate an orphanage for children whose parents had died of AIDS. Within Tanzania, as in any country, the evaluators from the university in Dar es Salaam differed in many ways from the people who lived in the rural town of the orphanage. Thus, they also sought extensive participation in planning, data collection, and interpretation from Tanzanians from that village and adjacent villages.

Finally, international work helps us to recognize some of the cultural and political contexts in our own countries and variations within our country, for example, across states and cities. Knowledge of international evaluations and the contextual elements that affect them can improve our own evaluations even if we never practice evaluation in another country. We become more sensitive to the larger contextual issues affecting our evaluations, for example, roles of government, evaluation policies and expectations for evaluation, styles of communicating, views concerning what constitutes credible evidence, and a variety of other contextual factors that affect our choices and the use of our findings. As Conner (2011) has observed, American evaluators could learn from treating our evaluations in the United States as if we were in a foreign country.

Closing

This chapter presents only a sampling of the evaluation literature that concerns context, but does delve into two areas, cross-cultural evaluation in the United States and international evaluation practice, which provide more depth on contextual factors than other areas. Other literature that alerts us to contextual elements we might otherwise overlook includes the literature on organizational learning (Preskill & Torres, 1998), the contexts of internal and external evaluators (Love, 1991; Sonnichsen, 1999), and differences across government, nonprofit, and private-sector programs (Davies, Newcomer, & Soydan, 2005). Our work here attempts to motivate readers to consider these and other elements of context, ones we might have overlooked. American evaluators (Frierson et al., 2002) recognize contextual differences across the cultures of racial and ethnic groups in the United States. The models of culturally responsive evaluation and standards on cultural competence come from their own contexts, evaluating youth at risk or underserved groups in a United States that has long been relatively heterogeneous. As such, they remind evaluators in other countries, countries with growing immigrant populations, to consider the cultural contexts of those served by the programs they are evaluating. Conversely, European evaluators are more likely to evaluate policies in many areas. Their knowledge of the contexts in which these programs and policies are developed, characteristics of government and policy making, and expectations of citizens regarding government can prompt American evaluators to consider these political contextual elements in their own work. We expand our awareness and improve our practice by moving beyond our own disciplinary and domestic boundaries to learn about how others consider and frame context.

References

American Evaluation Association. (2004). *Guiding principles for evaluators*. Retrieved from http://www.eval.org/Publications/GuidingPrinciples.asp

American Evaluation Association Policy Task Force. (2009). *An evaluation roadmap for a more effective government*. Retrieved from http://www.eval.org/aea09.eptf.eval.road mapF.pdf

Bamberger, M. (1999). Ethical issues in conducting evaluations in international settings. In J. Fitzpatrick & M. Morris (Eds.), *Current and emerging ethical challenges in evaluation. New Directions for Evaluation, 82,* 89–97.

Bhola, H. S. (2003). Social and cultural contexts of educational evaluation: A global perspective. In T. Kellaghan & D. L. Stufflebeam (Eds.), *International handbook of educational evaluation* (pp. 397–414). Dordrecht, Netherlands: Kluwer.

Chouinard, J. A., & Cousins, J. B. (2009). A review and synthesis of current research on cross-cultural evaluation. *American Journal of Evaluation, 30,* 457–494.

Christie, C. A. (2003). What guides evaluation? A study of how evaluation practice maps onto evaluation theory. In C. A. Christie (Ed.), *The practice–theory relationship in evaluation. New Directions for Evaluation, 97,* 7–36.

Conner, R. (2005). Multicultural evaluation. In S. Mathison (Ed.), *Encyclopedia of evaluation* (pp. 263–264). Thousand Oaks, CA: Sage.

Conner, R. (2011, November). *The effect of political values and expectations on evaluation: Perspectives from different countries.* Remarks as discussant for this session at the meeting of the American Evaluation Association, Anaheim, CA.

Cram, F. (2012, February 12). Remarks on American Evaluation's "Thought Leaders Forum."

Cram, F., Smith, L., & Johnstone, W. (2003). Mapping the themes of Māori talk about health. *New Zealand Medical Journal, 116.*

Dahler-Larsen, P., & Schwandt, T. A. (2012). Political culture as context for evaluation. In D. J. Rog, J. L. Fitzpatrick, & R. F. Conner (Eds.), *Context: A framework for its influence on evaluation practice. New Directions for Evaluation, 135,* pp. 75–87.

Davies, P., Newcomer, K., & Soydan, H. (2005). Government as structural context for evaluation. In I. F. Shaw, J. C. Greene, & M. M. Mark (Eds.), *The Sage handbook of evaluation* (pp. 163–183). London, United Kingdom: Sage.

Fitzpatrick, J. L., Christie, C. A., & Mark, M. M. (2009). *Evaluation in action: Interviews with expert evaluators.* Thousand Oaks, CA: Sage.

Fitzpatrick, J. L., Sanders, J. R., & Worthen, B. R. (2011). *Program evaluation: Alternative approaches and practical guidelines* (4th ed.). Upper Saddle River, NJ: Pearson.

Frierson, H., Hood, S., & Hughes, G. (2002). Strategies that address culturally responsive evaluation. In J. Frechtling (Ed.), *The 2002 user-friendly handbook for project evaluation* (pp. 63–73). Arlington, VA: National Science Foundation.

Greene, J. C. (2005). Context. In S. Mathison (Ed.), *Encyclopedia of evaluation* (pp. 82–84). Thousand Oaks, CA: Sage.

Greene, J. C., & Abma, T. A. (2001). Editors' notes. In J. C. Greene & T. A. Abma (Eds.), *Responsive evaluation. New Directions for Evaluation, 92,* 1–6.

Hood, S. (2001). Nobody knows my name: In praise of African American evaluators who were responsive. In J. C. Greene & T. A. Abma (Eds.), *Responsive evaluation. New Directions for Evaluation, 92,* 31–43.

Hood, S. (2005). Culturally-responsive evaluation. In S. Mathison (Ed.), *Encyclopedia of evaluation* (pp. 96–100). Thousand Oaks, CA: Sage.

Hood, S., Hopson, R., & Frierson, H. (Eds.) (2005). *The role of culture and cultural context: A mandate for inclusion, the discovery of truth and understanding in evaluation theory and practice.* Greenwich, CT: Information Age Publishing.

Hopson, R. (2009). Reclaiming knowledge at the margins: Culturally responsive evaluation in the current evaluation moment. In K. E. Ryan & J. B. Cousins (Eds.), *The Sage international handbook of educational evaluation* (pp. 429–446). Thousand Oaks, CA: Sage.

Horst, P., Nay, J. N., Scanlon, J. W., & Wholey, J. S. (1974). Program management and the federal evaluator. *Public Administration Review, 34,* 300–308.

Joint Committee on Standards for Educational Evaluation. (2011). *The program evaluation standards* (3rd ed.). Thousand Oaks, CA: Sage.

Kirkhart, K. E. (1995). Seeking multicultural validity: A postcard from the road. *Evaluation Practice, 16*(1), 1–12.

Love, A. J. (1991). *Internal evaluation: Building organizations from within.* Newbury Park, CA: Sage.

Madison, A. (2007). *New Directions for Evaluation* coverage of cultural issues and issues of significance to underrepresented groups. In S. Mathison (Ed.), *Enduring issues in evaluation: The 20th anniversary of collaboration between NDE and AEA. New Directions for Evaluation, 114,* 107–114.

McBride, D. F. (2011). Sociocultural theory: Providing more structure to culturally responsive evaluation. In S. Madison (Ed.), *Really new directions in evaluation: Young evaluators' perspectives. New Directions for Evaluation, No. 131,* 7–14.

Nevo, D. (1982). The international context for research on evaluation. *Evaluation News, 3*(4), 73–75.

Oxford University Press. (2010). *Oxford English language dictionary*. Retrieved from http://oxforddictionaries.com/definition/context?region=us

Patton, M. Q. (1976). *Utilization-focused evaluation*. Beverly Hills, CA: Sage.

Patton, M. Q., King, J., & Greenseid, L. (2007). The oral history of evaluation. Part V: An interview with Michael Quinn Patton. *American Journal of Evaluation, 28*, 102–114.

Pawson, R., & Tilley, N. (1997). *Realistic evaluation*. Thousand Oaks, CA: Sage.

Prado, J. (2011). "Honor the context": Opening lines for a critical multicultural evaluative practice. *American Journal of Evaluation, 32*, 418–427.

Preskill, H., & Torres, R. T. (1998). *Evaluative inquiry for learning in organizations*. Thousand Oaks, CA: Sage.

Rist, R. C. (Ed.). (1990). *Program evaluation and the management of government: Patterns and prospects across eight nations*. New Brunswick, NJ: Transaction Publishers.

Rog, D. J. (2012). When background becomes foreground: Toward context-sensitive evaluation practice. In D. J. Rog, J. L. Fitzpatrick, & R. F. Conner (Eds.), *Context: A framework for its influence on evaluation practice. New Directions for Evaluation, 135*, pp. 25–40.

SenGupta, S., Hopson, R., & Thompson-Robinson, M. (2004). Cultural competence in evaluation: An overview. In M. Thompson-Robinson, R. Hopson, & S. SenGupta (Eds.), *In search of cultural competence in evaluation. New Directions for Evaluation, 102*, pp. 5–15.

Shaw, I. F., Greene, J. C., & Mark, M. M. (Eds.). (2005). *The Sage handbook of evaluation*. London, United Kingdom: Sage.

Sonnichsen, R. C. (1999). *High impact internal evaluation*. Thousand Oaks, CA: Sage.

Stake, R. E. (1974). *Program evaluation, particularly responsive evaluation* (Occasional Paper No. 5). Kalamazoo: Western Michigan University Evaluation Center.

Stake, R. E. (1980). Program evaluation, particularly responsive evaluation. In W. B. Dockrell & D. Hamilton (Eds.), *Rethinking educational research*. London, United Kingdom: Hodeder & Stoughton.

Stern, E. (2005). Contextual challenges for evaluation practice. In I. F. Shaw, J. C. Greene, & M. M. Mark (Eds.), *The Sage handbook of evaluation* (pp. 292–314). London, United Kingdom: Sage.

Stevenson, J., & Thomas, D. (2005). Intellectual contexts. In I. F. Shaw, J. C. Greene, & M. M. Mark (Eds.), *The Sage handbook of evaluation* (pp. 200–224). London, United Kingdom: Sage.

Stufflebeam, D. L. (1968). *Evaluation as enlightenment for decision making*. Columbus: Ohio State University Evaluation Center.

Stufflebeam, D. L. (1971). The relevance of the CIPP evaluation model for educational accountability. *Journal of Research and Development in Education, 5*, 19–25.

Stufflebeam, D. L. (2007). *CIPP evaluation model checklist* (2nd ed.). Retrieved from http://www.wmich.edu/evalctr/archive_checklists/cippchecklist_mar07.pdf

Thomas, V. G. (2004). Building a contextually-responsive evaluation framework: Lessons from working with urban school interventions. In V. G. Thomas & F. I. Stevens (Eds.), *Co-constructing a contextually responsive evaluation framework: The talent development model of school reform. New Directions for Evaluation, 101*, 3–23.

Thompson-Robinson, M., Hopson, R., & SenGupta, S. (2004). Editors' notes. In M. Thompson-Robinson, R. Hopson, & S. SenGupta (Eds.), *In search of cultural competence in evaluation: Toward principles and practices. New Directions for Evaluation, 102*, 1–4.

Wallis, A., Dukay, V., & Fitzpatrick, J. (2008). Evaluation of Godfrey's Children Center in Tanzania. In J. Fitzpatrick, C. Christie, & M. M. Mark (Eds.), *Evaluation in action: Interviews with expert evaluators*. Thousand Oaks, CA: Sage.

Weiss, C. H. (1972). *Evaluation research: Methods for assessing program effectiveness*. Englewood Cliffs, NJ: Prentice-Hall.

Weiss, C. H. (1973). Where politics and evaluation research meet. *Evaluation, 1*, 37–45.
Wholey, J. S. (1979). *Evaluation: Promise and performance.* Washington, DC: Urban Institute.
Wholey, J. S. (1987). Evaluability assessment: Developing program theory. In L. Bickman (Ed.), *Using program theory in evaluation. New Directions for Evaluation, 33*, 77–92.

JODY L. FITZPATRICK *is associate professor in the school of public affairs at the University of Colorado, Denver, and will be the president of the American Evaluation Association in 2013.*

NEW DIRECTIONS FOR EVALUATION • DOI: 10.1002/ev

Rog, D. J. (2012). When background becomes foreground: Toward context-sensitive evaluation practice. In D. J. Rog, J. L. Fitzpatrick, & R. F. Conner (Eds.), *Context: A framework for its influence on evaluation practice. New Directions for Evaluation, 135,* 25–40.

2

When Background Becomes Foreground: Toward Context-Sensitive Evaluation Practice

Debra J. Rog

Abstract

This article aims to bring context from the background into the foreground of our work. Especially in more quantitative, outcome-focused efforts, context continues to play a character role. Though we recognize that context affects what we do and that it affects the programs and policies we study, the attention often is more implicit than explicit, and more as an afterthought when the work does not go as planned or findings are difficult to interpret. In this article, the goal is to give context more of a leading role by offering a framework for thinking about context and how we can enhance our practice by including an explicit focus on context in our evaluation inquiry. The article describes a strategy for context-sensitive practice that balances attention to context, stakeholder needs, and rigor. © Wiley Periodicals, Inc., and the American Evaluation Association.

C ontext matters. In evaluation, context shapes how we approach the work (i.e., the questions we address, the designs and methods we choose, the ways in which we report our findings). Context also affects the implementation and outcomes of the interventions that we study. Most theorists in our field have recognized the role that context plays in shaping our evaluations. For example, Patton (2008), in his utilization-focused evaluation approach, has stressed the importance of evaluators conducting a situational analysis to understand the decision and actor context as they embark on their evaluations. Nearly 40 years ago, Weiss (1973) sensitized us to the political context and how it affects how we think about use, and in extrapolation, how we disseminate and communicate our work to foster that use. Alkin (2004), in describing his context-adapted utilization approach, offers the perspective that although evaluators may use the various evaluation models that are available, they adapt them to each specific program context. As a psychologist, I can even go back to Kurt Lewin, the father of social psychology and action research, in his work on field theory (Lewin, 1943) and see that he recognized that behavior is affected by the physical and social elements that are in one's "life space" at a given time.

Despite the attention that theorists have given to context in evaluation, there is not a unified understanding of context or a comprehensive theory that guides our work. Greene (2005) notes that there is great variability among evaluation theories in how context is conceptualized, the various definitions and meanings it has, and how it operates within evaluation. She notes that more experimental, quantitative evaluators consider context a source of influence to be controlled, realist and theory-oriented theorists view it as a source of explanation, and qualitative theorists view it as an inseparable element that is embedded in program experiences and outcomes.

This chapter is aimed at bringing context from the background into the foreground of our work. Especially in more quantitative, outcome-focused efforts, context continues to play a character role. Though we recognize that context affects what we do and that it affects the programs and policies we study, the attention often is more implicit than explicit, and more of an afterthought when the work does not go as planned or findings emerge that are difficult to interpret. In this chapter, the goal is to give context more of a leading role by offering a framework for thinking about context and how we can enhance our practice by including an explicit focus on context in our evaluation inquiry.

The main thesis of this chapter is that context-sensitive evaluation practice may help guide us in our choice of an evaluation approach. As was discussed by contributors to an earlier *New Directions for Evaluation* issue on methods choice in government-sponsored evaluation (Julnes & Rog, 2007), there continues to be the need for productive dialogue on how best to match designs and methods to particular program and policy contexts to produce the most useful and actionable evidence. Context-sensitive evaluation eschews a methods-first orientation and suggests that a context-first approach for evaluation is more appropriate. The perspective is that the evaluator needs an understanding of which approaches to evaluation are most appropriate for particular contexts. Much like the question we strive to answer in our evaluations, "What works best for whom under what conditions?" context-sensitive evaluation practice asks "What evaluation approach provides the highest quality and most actionable evidence in which contexts?" (Mark, 2001). The answer to this question requires balancing, at a minimum, attention to context, stakeholder needs, and rigor. Accomplishing this balance likely entails understanding the many context issues that affect an evaluation and its evaluand, actively involving the range of stakeholders in the process, and drawing on a portfolio of methodological and analytic strategies to accommodate the context issues and needs in the most rigorous way possible (see Braverman, Engle, Arnold, & Rennekemp, 2008, for examples from cooperative extension service).

This chapter, and the 2009 American Evaluation Association Presidential Address on which it is based, were developed in the spirit of what Weiss refers to as "[l]earning from the field, learning in the field." My own evaluation experiences and those of other evaluation practitioners (e.g., Fitzpatrick, Christie, & Mark, 2009) informed the framework offered in the following pages. It begins by describing the different areas of context that can affect evaluation practice, followed by the role stakeholders can play in helping evaluators understand and appreciate the different dimensions within these various areas of context, and the methodological and analytic strategies available to attend to these dimensions more explicitly.

Areas of Context That Affect Evaluation Practice

As Greene (2005) notes, "Broadly speaking, context refers to the setting within which the evaluand (the program, policy, or product being evaluated) and thus the evaluation are situated. Context is the site, location, environment, or milieu for a given evaluand" (p. 85). She goes on to note that most evaluands operate in multiple contexts, most of which have several layers and dimensions.

In this section I highlight five areas of context to consider in conducting evaluations, from design through reporting findings. These contexts include the context of the problem or phenomenon being addressed, the context of the intervention being examined, the broader environment or setting in which the intervention is being studied, the parameters of the evaluation itself, and the broader decision-making context. In each of these context areas, there are dimensions to examine—the physical, organizational, social, cultural, tradition, political, and historical (see Figure 2.1). As others have noted, some of these dimensions need to be unpacked further; within the social and cultural dimensions; for example, SenGupta, Hopson, and Thompson-Robinson (2004) note that we need to look not only at demographic issues of gender, race, and language, but also other dimensions we often ignore, such as power differences, class, other denominators of equity, and sociopolitical status. Each of these areas of context is reviewed in the following sections.

The Phenomenon and the Problem

The nature of the phenomenon and problem can be critical in choosing an approach to evaluation, yet it is the least referenced in evaluators' discussions

Figure 2.1. Areas of Context That Affect Evaluation Practice

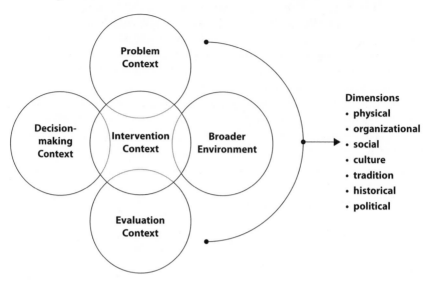

of context. In addition to the specific nature of the phenomenon, other dimensions of the problem context that affect one's evaluation approach include how much is already known about the problem, the types of studies that have been conducted, and the tools and other data that might be available to incorporate into the evaluation. Knowing more about the nature of the problem, its extent, the circumstances in which it exists, which populations are affected, and so on, can be essential to scoping out and implementing an evaluation approach that is appropriate to this context area.

Let me offer an illustration from my work in evaluating interventions for homeless adults and homeless families. In the early to mid 1980s, a new era of homelessness was just coming onto the horizon (e.g., Rossi, 1990). Because of the crisis and emergency nature of the problem at the time, interventions often were developed relatively quickly without being intensely developed or informed by a research base. Some of these early efforts consequently were hampered by the absence of a detailed theory of action. For example, in a large-scale evaluation of housing and service programs for homeless families beginning in 1990, the program's aim was to create systems change but there was no explicit theory of how the projects were to make this happen. Moreover, there was not a detailed understanding of what even constituted a system for homeless families or what to measure as the outcomes of systems change (Fitzpatrick, 1999; Rog & Gutman, 1997). A controlled study in this instance would have been ill advised, as it would not have been able to be mounted with integrity because of the dynamics of the problem, nor would it likely have produced the type of effects that could be detected. Therefore, the design was a descriptive one, with both qualitative and quantitative data collection and several longitudinal components to track the implementation of the program and changes that were occurring. Because so little was known about the characteristics, needs, and experiences of homeless families, we built in study components that helped to add to the field's understanding of the problem of homelessness and the individuals experiencing it. We knew we could not have a controlled understanding of the intervention and its effects, but we could build our understanding of the context of the problem through information on the population, the program, and the system. In this instance, therefore, we chose to be design poor, but data rich.

The Nature of the Intervention

The structure, complexity, and dynamics in the program situation affect the selection and implementation of an evaluation approach. The stage of the program (i.e., where it is in its life cycle), for example, has great implications for the type of evaluation that makes sense. In addition, how dynamic and evolving a program is, how complex it is with respect to its theory of change, and the extent to which it blurs with the setting itself are all factors to consider in choosing evaluation designs and methods.

Environmental interventions are good examples of complex programs requiring methodological creativity and adaptation (see Birnbaum & Mickwitz, 2009). They typically involve both social and physical processes as well as incorporate efforts targeted to the economic and structural elements of the problem (e.g., recycling). In addition, there often is a blurring of the intervention within the broader environment, making it difficult to make attributions of change to the intervention because of the number of confounding externalities (take the example of interventions to reduce climate change). In some instances, it may be possible to measure the effects of an intervention, but it is hard to trace the exact causal mechanism or mechanisms. As Thurston, Smith, Genskow, Prokopy, and Hargrove (2012) note in Chapter 3 of this issue, these intervention effects often take many years to occur, requiring interim measures sensitive to showing that the intervention is making changes in the short-run that indicate it is on the right track. Finally, as with many areas of intervention, the area of environmental intervention involves a range of stakeholders with diverse and often conflicting beliefs, values, and assumptions. As a consequence of all these challenges, evaluations of environmental interventions need to have multiple indicators, multiple methods, and often need to examine multiple pathways to see if and how change occurs.

The Broader Environment/Setting

The environment or setting in which a program is situated is what evaluators most commonly view as the context surrounding a program. In many cases, as Greene (2005) writes, this area of context is multilayered; she provides an example of educational interventions that are situated within classrooms but are also affected by the broader environments of the school, the school district, the broader community, and the state. In addition, as noted above, some programs and initiatives blur with the broader environment. Community change efforts, for example, are intertwined with the communities in which they are taking place (Rog & Knickman, 2004).

Currently, I am directing a multisite evaluation of a large-scale initiative to change county systems of services for homeless families from an orientation of managing homelessness to ending homelessness. In this effort, there is no clear distinction between the intervention and the system. Looking across systems in three different counties, we may be able to identify components to the intervention that are present in each model implementation, but there are also likely to be modifications and adaptations to the model to meet the specific needs of each community. However, because the initiative is guided by a theory of change that articulates a progression of outcomes across a longitudinal time frame, we are able to use that theory in developing a specific set of measures to track changes. In addition, we are building into the design two contrast communities that do not have the intervention, but are likely engaging in some type of systems activity because of a more general national push to end homelessness as we know it. By having these two contrast counties in the study, we are able to compare and contrast patterns of intervention and outcome and perhaps more clearly distinguish the initiative's effect from those produced by efforts within communities, the state, and the federal government.

It also is important to understand the ways in which the broader environment affects the ability of an intervention to achieve outcomes. For example, the outcomes of an intervention designed to assist homeless individuals in accessing housing are moderated by the extent to which there is sufficient affordable housing available. A strong, well-developed intervention may work well in a housing market where there is a high vacancy rate, but may not be able to achieve outcomes in a tight housing market. Understanding the role context plays is thus critical to understanding the generalizability of the evaluation findings to other contexts and situations.

The Evaluation Context

Several evaluators have written about the context with respect to the parameters for the evaluation. The budget, time, and the data available for the evaluation all influence method choice. Bamberger and colleagues (Bamberger, Rugh, & Mabry, 2006), for example, have proposed strategies for designing international outcome studies that explicitly address these constraints in an effort to maximize validity and overall quality and use. As an example, the authors describe situations in development evaluation where change data are desired, yet there are no baseline data available. They outline strategies

NEW DIRECTIONS FOR EVALUATION • DOI: 10.1002/ev

for reconstructing baseline data, such as through recall and/or with secondary data, and discuss the advantages and disadvantages of each strategy in particular situations.

When I worked for a state legislative oversight agency, we were constantly asked to conduct rigorous outcome-focused studies in very short time frames. We understood that the legislature needed to make go or no-go decisions for some programs and wanted the best information available to guide those decisions. Matching methods to the context to produce data that would be actionable, however, at times meant reworking the evaluation questions with the key decision makers.

As an example, the legislature had funded a diversion program for nonviolent offenders in the state that was intended to reduce recidivism and, in turn, reduce prison overcrowding and costs. After 18 months of funding, the legislature asked for an evaluation of the outcomes of the program. Was the program working and was it reducing recidivism? Was it reducing costs? An 18-month time period, however, was not sufficient to conduct a sensitive test of recidivism. We engaged in an interchange with the key legislative committee and determined that, based on the time frame, we could not address the ultimate outcome question, but we could examine if the program was on track for reducing costs. Was it serving the folks it was intended to serve? Because judges determined whether an offender would be sentenced to the diversion program or to incarceration or probation, we could conduct a study to see if the profiles of those who were being sentenced to the program were more like those who were typically incarcerated or those who were put on probation. If the profiles looked more like offenders who were incarcerated, then we would conclude that judges were using the program as an alternative to incarceration, and it had the possibility of decreasing costs. If, however, the profiles of those in the diversion program looked more like offenders who were being placed on probation, the program was probably not on track, and was likely costing more than expected.

We conducted a set of analyses with the use of sentencing data and found that the majority of offenders sentenced to the program mirrored the profile of offenders who would otherwise be incarcerated (Rog & Henry, 1987); they were primarily individuals who had committed burglary. Overall, we concluded that the program was being implemented as expected and had the potential to save money. For the immediate decision-making context, there was sufficient strong evidence to support keeping the program as is and measuring the longer-term outcomes of recidivism in the future.

Decision-Making Context

As the example above illustrates, in choosing methods that can maximally attend to the needs of the decision-making context, it is important to understand who

NEW DIRECTIONS FOR EVALUATION • DOI: 10.1002/ev

the decision makers are, the types of decisions they need to make, the standards of rigor they expect, and the level of confidence that is needed to make the decision, as well as other structural and cultural factors that influence their behavior (e.g., Braverman et al., 2008). For example, in the book *Foundations and Evaluation* (Braverman, Constantine, & Slater, 2004), much was written about the need for evaluators to understand and adapt to the structural and cultural factors that influence a foundation's grant giving and evaluation. Understanding the funding and decision cycles, the purposes the foundation has for evaluation, and the location of action and responsibility for evaluation are all viewed as critical for evaluators in designing and conducting evaluations that can be useful in this context. In addition, understanding the decision-making context can influence not only the selection of an evaluation approach, but also the ways in which results and recommendations are communicated (e.g., Iriti, Bickel, & Nelson, 2005).

Attending to and Involving Stakeholders to Increase Context Sensitivity

Involving stakeholders in the evaluation process, especially those directly affected by the problem and involved in the program, can heighten evaluators' sensitivity to the areas of context described above. Consumers or beneficiaries of a program can provide an unparalleled perspective on the problem, the intervention, and the broader environment that may help to guide designs that are more feasible, measurement that is more focused, and interpretations that offer new insights. In a multisite evaluation of services for homeless families, women across the sites who had experienced homelessness worked closely with the evaluators in designing the study. Their involvement in designing the data-collection tools gave us insights that we would likely not have had without their involvement. For example, our study Steering Committee's interest in examining trauma in detail and thus proposing multiple instruments within our protocol that we all reviewed together for an extended period of time led to several of the women having their past trauma retriggered. Their experiences led us not only to reduce our data-collection focus in this area, but also to institute a safety plan to accompany the interview in the event interviewees experience retraumatization.

Involvement of a range of stakeholders, especially beneficiaries, builds in responsiveness to possible social justice issues. In particular, it can help to ensure that the way the study is conducted and how the data are presented do not further disenfranchise those who are the focus of an evaluation, especially if they are among the least advantaged. In addition, involving consumers in different aspects of a study can foster transparency of methods, reveal flaws and suggest study qualifications, and in turn help to promote study findings as credible and having integrity.

Using a Range of Methods to Accommodate and Incorporate Context

In conducting context-sensitive evaluation, evaluators will need to avail themselves of a portfolio of methodological and analytic strategies that can accommodate and address the variety of context issues that arise. Our array of design, data collection, and analysis tools continues to grow and strengthens our ability to produce actionable evidence in a range of evaluation situations. Three sets of strategies are highlighted in this section: analytic strategies that help us infer causality, specifically in ruling in or ruling out alternative explanations; techniques for improving the accuracy of the estimates of program effects in a range of evaluation designs; and strategies for enhancing the explanatory power of our studies by explicitly incorporating context into the evaluation.

Strategies to Rule In or Rule Out Alternative Explanations

There are strategies that enhance the ability of nonexperimental and quasi-experimental studies to establish causality and rule out alternative explanations when the randomized study is not possible or desirable. In her book *The Nuts and Bolts of Sound Evaluation*, Davidson (2005) offers eight practical strategies for inferring causation for evaluation situations ranging in the level of certainty needed, the level of resources, and other factors that influence the designs possible. One of the strategies, for example, is based on Scriven's modus operandi method (1974), and involves looking for signature traces or telltale patterns in the data by examining chains of causal events.

Another strategy to enhance nonexperimental studies involves conducting a systematic plausibility analysis of the threats to validity. This requires not only collecting data on the theory of change that an intervention may be following, but also data on the plausibility of rival explanations. In a pre–post multisite study of housing and services for families in the child welfare system, we conducted a plausibility analysis of the likely threats by examining patterns in the findings across the sites (see Rog, Mongelli, & Lundy, 1998). At AEA's 2007 conference in Baltimore, Jack McKillip and his colleagues (McKillip, Rycraft, Wernet, Patchner, & Mech, 2007) described their efforts to strengthen an evaluation of a training program for health and pregnancy counseling professionals through the use of plausibility analysis. In this study, they used the pretest–posttest-only design, a design that is commonly recognized as open to many threats to validity. The evaluators collected data and conducted secondary analyses on each of the plausible threats: history, testing, and instrumentation. They were able to examine the effects of testing or practice efforts, for example, by varying whether individuals in different training sessions had one, two, or no pretests. They also varied the doses of the treatment, 3-day versus 1-day trainings, and were able to show training effects that were larger for the 3-day versus 1-day training. Other between-session variance in training effects was very small, suggesting that history was not accounting for the effects. The researchers in this effort, therefore, built into their design an a priori plausibility analysis. Although they could not control the threats to validity, they collected targeted information that allowed them to explain the extent to which the threats were operating to confound the results.

Techniques for Improving the Accuracy of the Estimates of Program Effects

A second set of strategies to improve the quality of evidence produced by evaluation in a range of contexts is focused on improving or sharpening the accuracy of the estimates of the effects from outcome studies, especially nonexperimental and quasiexperimental approaches. Some of these strategies occur at the design stage, others at the analysis stage.

First, there appears to be a resurgence of the use of evaluability assessment (Rog, 2005; Trevisan, 2005), a method developed by Joe Wholey and colleagues in the 1970s (Wholey, 1979). Evaluability assessment was designed to determine the extent to which a program or policy is ready for an outcome evaluation, the changes that are needed in a program to increase its readiness, and the type of evaluation approach most suitable to judge a program or policy's performance. Evaluability assessment helps to ensure that the program to be evaluated has an internal logic that is implemented with integrity so that the outcomes as specified are plausible to achieve. Although it has typically focused more on program logic and the needs of stakeholders, evaluability assessment also is particularly well suited to understanding how a program fits within the broader environment, the features of the environment that may moderate the effects of the program, and how the evaluation may need to be structured to be maximally sensitive to this area of context. It can guide the development of tools and strategies for more explicitly examining features within the layers of context in the broader environment, such as the organizational context and the community context, that may influence the program's operations and affect its outcomes.

A second design strategy that can help sharpen the accuracy of estimates of effects from outcome studies, especially in multisite studies, is a focus on fidelity of the intervention to its intended model (e.g., Summerfelt, 2003). Understanding fidelity and implementation level, especially how a program is interacting with the broader environment, is important for either selecting programs for outcome assessment or incorporating the fidelity data into analyses to test for the moderating effects of fidelity.

At the analysis stage, several techniques have been developed to strengthen the accuracy of estimates of effects from nonexperimental and quasiexperimental studies. These include developing comparison groups through statistical matching techniques such as propensity scores (e.g., Rubin, 1997), and matching groups on pretest scores. In addition, for even relatively weak outcome designs such as the pre–post design, having an estimate of the size of the effect, such as the U3 measure (the percentage of posttests above the median on the pretest), as used by McKillip and colleagues (2007) in their study of the training program, helps to bound the results and offer more information on change. In addition, technical efforts such as this and the work on case studies of comprehensive reforms (Yin & Davis, 2007) and single-subject designs to extend meta-analytic logic to a range of other designs (Shadish & Rindskopf, 2007) also help not only to understand the level of impact in a single study, but in a body of literature.

Strategies for Improving the Explanatory Power of Our Studies

Finally, we can strengthen our ability to produce actionable evidence by using strategies that enhance the explanatory power of our studies. This often means adding methods, both qualitative and quantitative, to our outcome studies that go beyond determining whether a program works or not to explore why the outcomes occur or fail to occur. This can include elaborating our theories to include potential mediators in a program that link activities with outcomes and testing for them in our analyses. A perspective on actionable evidence also recognizes that because many outcomes are multiply determined, an evaluation needs to build in opportunities to test for patterns of effects.

Here is where the focus centers on context in evaluation. Attending to how context affects the implementation and outcomes of the programs we study may enhance our evaluations and in turn strengthen our ability to provide stronger actionable evidence. So, much like we have opened the black box of programs and provided useful data on the role that program mechanisms can have in triggering outcomes, I hope we can also navigate and explore the black hole of context and determine which aspects and areas of context have a role in determining the successes or failures of the interventions.

Integrating contextual variables within the evaluation inquiry as a source of explanatory influences is a key aspect of the realist evaluation approach (Henry, Julnes, & Mark, 1998; Pawson & Tilley, 1997). The realist approach goes beyond determining whether a program works or not to explaining the consequences of social actions that contribute to a better understanding of why, where, and for whom programs work or fail to work. The emphasis is on identifying the mechanisms and contextual variables that moderate the effects. This approach acknowledges that programs are embedded in the layers of social realities that we spoke about earlier and that measurement of these variables will provide more valid evidence of program outcomes.

There are analytic tools that also can help us assess the role of context in our evaluations. Social network analysis (e.g., Durland & Fredericks, 2006) is offering a different lens for evaluators than traditionally used and may provide a method for helping us embrace systematically the effects of influences on program participants that are outside the program and in their broader environment. This is part of the systems thinking development that is becoming more prominent. For example, Patton (2011) provides an example of an evaluation of a pregnancy prevention program in describing developmental evaluation. A typical logic model would display the activities of the program and their desired outcomes for the program participants, young teen girls. However, with a broader systems approach in which context is explicitly considered, the model might incorporate the other influences that are assumed to be operating, such as the role of peers, the role of families, the role of church, the role of media, and even the roles of other interventions (as so often occurs with social services). The study could incorporate each of these factors in the data collection, including how they impact the participants, the program's effects (either strengthening or lessening them), and one another.

In addition, evaluators traditionally focus on measures of central tendency in analyzing and reporting findings, statistics that may not be sensitive to the differences that often result from complex, dynamic interventions, especially those serving heterogeneous populations in equally dynamic settings. Greater sensitivity and explanatory power can be gained by going beyond "averages" to understanding variation, with greater attention to distributions of outcomes and to patterns of change. For example, in a recent study of homeless families participating in mental health and substance abuse programs, examining outcomes over time found no significant differences between families served in the target interventions and those who received services as usual in the community. Improvement over time was the average pattern of change across the two groups. However, with the use of group-based trajectory analysis (Nagin, 2005; Nagin & Odgers, 2010) on the total sample of families in the study, we found three to five distinct patterns of change on each of the outcomes. In general, there was a group of families that started out at a low level of an outcome and improved over time (much like the overall finding), a group that appeared not to need the services at all (starting out and staying at a positive level), and a group that started out at a very poor level and did not improve at all. These different patterns of change related to other changes that were occurring in the context of families' lives that helped to identify subgroups that may require different intervention approaches. For example, ongoing trauma in a woman's life was having more impact on the outcomes than her participation in a program. Identifying these subgroups helps to inform different intervention approaches and provides actionable evidence for practitioners and policy makers.

Finally, multisite studies offer an advantage to measure the influences of the broader environment on programs. In a study of the SAMHSA ACCESS program for individuals who are homeless and have mental illness (Rosenheck et al., 2001), the evaluators examined the relationship among several variables, including characteristics of the social environment (social capital, housing affordability), the level of service integration in each system, individual client access to and use of services, and client outcomes (successful exit from homelessness and clinical improvement). Both of the contextual variables tested, social capital and housing affordability, influenced housing outcomes, through direct and indirect pathways, but neither related to clinical outcomes. This analysis provided an understanding of the impact of the community context on client outcomes.

We can extend the type of context measurement used in multisite studies to single evaluations as well. Although the use of these variables in a single study is more descriptive, if we continue to bring it to the foreground in our studies and focus on some of the same general areas, we would be able to enrich our meta-analyses and syntheses in an intervention or problem area and across areas. Just as we have delved into the black box of interventions and have incorporated dosage measures and program measures of implementation in our examinations of the outcomes of program, so might we consider delving more systematically into the role that context plays. How we measure and incorporate context measures in each evaluation will likely have various levels and focus on relevant aspects of the each area of context (political, cultural, social, organizational). Clearly, there are limits to what we can do and we need to be judicious with our resources. Not all interventions are as susceptible to their contexts and not all investigations have to study each area of context with the same level of rigor and intensity used to study the core elements of a program and the outcomes. Yet it may be helpful to have a heightened awareness of the role that context can and does play, and to embrace it more directly in our evaluations. Explicit measurement of the context may not only enrich the explanation for the evaluation, but may provide more direction in replication and generalizability of the findings.

Actionable Evidence

I have advocated for gearing studies to the needs of the decision-making context so that actionable evidence can be produced. The other perspective that needs to be considered is how the evidence fits within the broader needs of a field and for the public as a whole. We are becoming increasingly cognizant that the work we do in any single evaluation should have cumulative force. Single studies are rarely definitive, but often fit within a broader literature. Attention to the contextual elements of the study may help to make the findings more generalizable.

In the area in which I work, homelessness, much of what we have learned about the population as well as the interventions comes from evaluation studies. All of the studies have flaws in one way or another, but are often considered together in assessing what we know at this stage in the dilemma. Some of the early work I did in the 1990s (e.g., Rog & Gutman,1997) continues to have weight in the body of evidence around the importance of subsidized supportive housing for families. Each time another study confirms the findings of that initial study on family supportive housing, it receives renewed importance.

In addition, although some of the analysis of context in a single study will be descriptive, if we continue to bring it to the foreground in our studies and focus on some of the same areas across studies, we will enrich our meta-analyses and syntheses in an intervention area and across intervention areas.

Final Plea

I would like to end with a plea and a challenge. We have progressed so far in the 30 years since I entered this field. The sophistication and relevance of our evaluation approaches has improved and our influence in some circles has increased. As a field we have exploded, with more than 6,000 members of AEA at last count and societies and networks in place across the globe. However, much of our growth has happened without careful study of our work. We need more study of evaluation practice itself; we need to accumulate knowledge about evaluation. So I challenge those of you who may be early in your careers to begin this pathway to studying ourselves more critically and begin to develop an empirical base on the effectiveness of our choices of designs, methods, and other aspects of our work. The course over the next 30 years should be guided by the data on what works in our practice so that the debate over the primacy of certain methods and a methods-first orientation will be replaced by one that is focused on context first and increasing our chances of making a difference through our work.

References

Alkin, M. (2004). Context adapted utilization: A personal journey. In M. Alkin (Ed.), *Evaluation roots: Tracing theorists' views and influences.* Thousand Oaks, CA: Sage.

Bamberger, M., Rugh, J., & Mabry, L. (2006). *Real world evaluation: Working under budget, time, data, and political constraints.* Thousand Oaks, CA: Sage.

Birnbaum, M., & Mickwitz, P. (Eds). (2009). *Environmental program and policy evaluation: Addressing methodological challenges. New Directions for Evaluation, 122.*

Braverman, M. T., Constantine, N. A., & Slater, J. K. (Eds.) (2004). *Foundations and evaluation: Contexts and practices for effective philanthropy.* San Francisco, CA: Jossey-Bass.

Braverman, M. T., Engle, M., Arnold, M. E., & Rennekemp, R. A. (Eds.). (2008). *Program evaluation in a complex organizational system: Lessons from cooperative extension. New Directions for Evaluation, 120.*

Davidson, E. J. (2005). *Evaluation methodology basics: The nuts and bolts of sound evaluation.* Thousand Oaks, CA: Sage.

Durland, M. M., & Fredericks, K. A. (Eds.). (2006). *Social network analysis in program evaluation. New Directions for Evaluation, 107.*

Fitzpatrick, J. (1999). Dialogue with Debra J. Rog. *American Journal of Evaluation, 20,* 562–575.

Fitzpatrick, J., Christie, C., & Mark, M. (2009). *Evaluation in action: Interviews with expert evaluators.* Thousand Oaks, CA: Sage.

Greene, J. (2005). Context. In S. Mathison (Ed.), *Encyclopedia of evaluation.* Thousand Oaks, CA: Sage.

Henry, G., Julnes, G. J., & Mark, M. (Eds.). (1998). *Realist evaluation.* San Francisco, CA: Jossey Bass.

Iriti, J. E., Bickel, W. E., & Nelson, C. A. (2005). Using recommendations in evaluation: A decision-making framework for evaluators. *American Journal of Evaluation, 26*(4), 464–479.

Julnes, G., & Rog, D. J. (Eds.). (2007). *Informing federal policies on evaluation methodology: Building the evidence base for method choice in government sponsored evaluations. New Directions for Evaluation, 113.*

Lewin, K. (1943). Defining the "field at a given time." *Psychological Review, 50,* 292–310.

Mark, M. M. (2001). Evaluation's future: Furor, futile, or fertile? *American Journal of Evaluation, 22,* 457–479.

McKillip, J., Rycraft, J., Wernet, S., Patchner, M., & Mech, E. (2007). *Using the pretest/post-test only design for evaluation of training.* Presented at the annual meeting of the American Evaluation Association, Baltimore, MD.

Nagin, D. S. (2005). *Group-based modeling of development.* Cambridge, MA: Harvard University Press.

Nagin, D. S., & Odgers, C. L. (2010). Group-based trajectory modeling in clinical research. *Annual Review of Clinical Psychology, 6,* 109–138.

Patton, M. Q. (2008). *Utilization-focused evaluation* (4th ed.). Thousand Oaks, CA: Sage.

Patton, M. Q. (2011). *Developmental evaluation: Appling complexity concepts to enhance innovation and use.* New York, NY: Guilford Press.

Pawson, R., & Tilley, N. (1997). *Realistic evaluation.* Thousand Oaks, CA: Sage.

Rog, D. J. (2005, October). *Evaluability assessment: Then and now.* Presented at the Joint Meeting of the Canadian Evaluation Society and the American Evaluation Association, Toronto, Ontario, Canada.

Rog, D. J., & Gutman, M. (1997). The Homeless Families Program: A summary of key findings. In S. L. Isaacs & J. R. Knickman (Eds.), *The Robert Wood Johnson Foundation anthology: To improve health and health care* (pp. 209–231). San Francisco, CA: Jossey-Bass.

Rog, D. J., & Henry, G. T. (1987). An implementation evaluation of community corrections. *Evaluation Review, 11,* 337–354.

Rog, D. J., & Knickman, J. R. (2004). Strategies for comprehensive initiatives. In M. T. Braverman, N. A. Constantine, & J. K. Slater (Eds.), *Foundations and evaluation: Contexts and practices for effective philanthropy.* San Francisco, CA: Jossey-Bass.

Rog, D. J., Mongelli, A. G., & Lundy, E. (1998). *The Family Unification Program: Final evaluation report.* Washington, DC: CWLA Press.

Rosenheck, R., Morrissey, J., Lam, J., Calloway, M., Stolar, M., Johnsen, M., . . . Goldman, H. (2001). Service delivery and community: Social capital, service systems integration, and outcomes among homeless persons with severe mental illness. *Health Services Research, 36,* 691–710.

Rossi, P. (1990). *Down and out in America: The origins of homelessness.* Chicago, IL: University of Chicago Press.

Rubin, D. (1997). Estimating causal effects from large data sets using propensity scores. *Annals of Internal Medicine, 127,* 757–763.

Scriven, M. (1974). Evaluation perspectives and procedures. In W. J. Popham (Ed.), *Evaluation in education.* Berkeley, CA: McCutchan.

SenGupta, S., Hopson, R., & Thompson-Robinson, M. (2004). Cultural competence in evaluation: An overview. In M. Thompson-Robinson, R. Hopson, & S. SenGupta (Eds.), *In search of cultural competence in evaluation: Toward principles and practices. New Directions for Evaluation, 102,* 5–19.

Shadish, W., & Rindskopf, D. M. (2007). Methods for evidence-based practice: Quantitative synthesis of single-subject designs. In G. Julnes & D. J. Rog (Eds.), *Informing federal policies on evaluation methodology: Building the evidence base for method choice in government-sponsored evaluation. New Directions for Evaluation, 113,* 75–94.

Summerfelt, T. (2003). Program strength and fidelity in evaluation. *Applied Developmental Science, 7,* 55–61.

Thurston, L. P., Smith, C. A., Genskow, K., Prokopy, L. S., & Hargrove, W. L. (2012). The social context of water quality improvement evaluation. In D. J. Rog, J. L. Fitzpatrick, & R. F. Conner (Eds.), *Context: A framework for its influence on evaluation practice. New Directions for Evaluation, 135,* 41–58.

Trevisan, M. S. (2005, October). *The methodology and practice of evaluability assessment: 1985–2004.* Paper presented at the Annual Meeting of the American Evaluation Association, Toronto, Ontario, Canada.

Weiss, C. H. (1973). Where politics and evaluation research meet. *Evaluation,* 37–45.

Wholey, J. S. (1979). *Evaluation: Promise and performance.* Washington, DC: The Urban Institute.

Yin, R. K., & Davis, D. (2007). Adding new dimensions to case study evaluations: The case of evaluating comprehensive reforms. In G. Julnes & D. J. Rog (Eds.), *Informing federal policies on evaluation methodology: Building the evidence base for method choice in government-sponsored evaluation. New Directions for Evaluation, 113,* 75–94.

DEBRA J. ROG is an associate director at Westat and president of The Rockville Institute. She was the 2009 president of the American Evaluation Association.

Thurston, L. P., Smith, C. A., Genskow, K., Prokopy, L. S., & Hargrove, W. L. (2012). The social context of water quality improvement evaluation. In D. J. Rog, J. L. Fitzpatrick, & R. F. Conner (Eds.), *Context: A framework for its influence on evaluation practice. New Directions for Evaluation, 135,* 41–58.

3

The Social Context of Water Quality Improvement Evaluation

Linda P. Thurston, Christa A. Smith, Kenneth Genskow, Linda Stalker Prokopy, William L. Hargrove

Abstract

The complexity of physical and social contexts for water resource management presents considerable problems for designing, implementing, and evaluating interventions for water quality and quantity problems. Water resource management is increasingly being conducted on a watershed scale, where watersheds are areas of land that drain into the same water body. Deborah Rog's model of context-sensitive evaluation provides a framework for understanding and addressing the complexity of watersheds and watershed management, restoration, and protection. This chapter discusses the problems inherent in evaluating watershed projects. It presents three overarching considerations for evaluating these types of projects: diversity of stakeholder groups, complexity of identifying and measuring outcomes, and evaluation ethos. Finally, the chapter stresses the need for specifically evaluating the social dimensions of watershed projects and provides an example of a water quality evaluation that addresses regional social indicators. Rog's five areas of context are described in this example. © Wiley Periodicals, Inc., and the American Evaluation Association.

W ater quantity and quality are global issues of increasing importance. In his book *Dry Spring* (Wood, 2008), Chris Wood documents dramatic and significant instances of unprecedented excess and scarcity of water in the United States. The development and evaluation of interventions related to water quantity and quality are typified by a unique set of characteristics that illustrate the role of context in evaluation. The geophysical, geopolitical, and behavioral aspects of watersheds and the use of watersheds as the focal point to water quality issues present interesting challenges to evaluators. Rog's (2012) model of context-sensitive evaluation provides intervention and policy planners as well as evaluators with a framework for understanding and addressing the complexity of watersheds and watershed management, restoration, and protection. This chapter will discuss the contextual issues related to evaluating water quality programs in the United States with a focus on the problem and setting contexts of Rog's model. We first describe the history and meaning of watershed approaches to water quantity and quality problems, and then discuss the problem context in which water quality programs are evaluated, focusing on three specific contextual variables. Finally, an initiative aimed at developing social indicators for water quality management and evaluation is presented within the framework of Rog's five context areas: problem, setting, intervention, evaluation, and decision making.

The Watershed Approach to Water Quality

Issues related to water quality and quantity are framed by environmental agencies in the context of watersheds. Simply, a watershed is an area of land that catches rain and snow and then drains into a body of water like a marsh, stream, river, or lake. Watersheds are nested and hierarchical. All activities within a watershed have the potential to impact that watershed's water quality and the quantity of water available. Watersheds may also be called *catchments* or *basins*. Because they define the geographical boundaries of a hydrological system, they are often used as the framework for analysis and management of water issues. They are often the basis for efforts to integrate water management activities (Hooper et al., 1999; Margerum, 1999; U.S. Environmental Protection Agency [USEPA], 1996). This watershed approach to address water quality problems thus defines the solution as developing and implementing effective, comprehensive programs for water protection, restoration, and management.

The watershed approach to address water quality problems means that the focus is on a watershed, not a county or a state or any organized unit. Watersheds cross jurisdictional lines, adding greatly to the complexity of governance and of developing (and evaluating) interventions for water quality protection and restoration. The human use of the geographic space contained within watersheds can widely vary and includes agricultural production, recreational activities, and urban dwellings. Stakeholders for water quality interventions can be anyone dependent on clean water or whose actions affect the water resources. The diversity of stakeholders is inherent in the watershed approach. Beyond the audiences of individual landowners targeted for water quality interventions, stakeholders can include local agricultural interests, representatives of wastewater treatment plants and other regulated dischargers, and environmental groups. The interaction of these factors and many others illustrates the complexity and intricacy of watershed systems.

Actions taken on lands across a watershed can combine to create cumulative negative impacts on water quality, habitat, and overall ecological health. Dislocation of soil from agricultural or construction practices, excessive nutrients from fertilizers and animal wastes, or increased water volume during storm events due to newly paved surfaces and development all contribute to local, regional, and national water quality problems. Water management agencies refer to these pollutants as *runoff, diffuse,* or *nonpoint sources* (NPS) of water quality impairment. Local problems might include silted reservoirs, oxygen-depleting algal blooms, fish kills, or contaminated drinking water. At the regional and national levels, cumulative excessive nutrients are leading to hypoxia (dead zones) in the Gulf of Mexico and the Chesapeake Bay.

Efforts for controlling those problematic diffuse sources have relied heavily on voluntary approaches that incentivize action by individuals. Although there are regulatory programs for municipal and industrial dischargers (including large operations for animal agriculture), over the past three decades many federal, state, and private programs have focused primarily on voluntary efforts. These voluntary programs generally offer educational, technical, and financial assistance to encourage the use of various management practices, called *best management practices* (or BMPs), that are expected to reduce negative impacts on water quality. Examples of BMPs are physical changes, such as constructing a rain garden infiltration area or manure storage pit, or nonstructural activities such as developing (and using) nutrient management plans for agricultural operations, changing crop varieties, or changing timing and amounts of lawn chemical applications.

Problem Context: Description of the Problem of Water Quality Improvement Evaluation

The hydrological necessity of using watersheds as operational units presents challenges to those working on water quality planning, policy, and evaluation. This approach to watershed protection and restoration calls for the development and evaluation of management plans by multiple stakeholders as described above. Watershed protection and restoration involves measuring biophysical factors for the purposes of accountability and adherence to regulations. It also involves attention to sociopolitical factors such as regulations and policies, attitudes about water ownership and use, shared resources and collaboration, and individual behaviors.

As noted, watersheds are hierarchical, and the problem defines the space of the watershed, encompassing governmental and social boundaries

NEW DIRECTIONS FOR EVALUATION • DOI: 10.1002/ev

(Bruyninckx, 2009). The scale of a watershed includes all pollutant sources (end of pipe and diffuse) generated from multiple uses or functions for the land and water. Controlling diffuse/NPS pollution is one of the most challenging water quality management issues. Interventions implemented at different sites can generate different results, which further complicates and enhances our understanding of what types of interventions work under what types of conditions. The importance of scalability of interventions is also an important consideration. There are challenges inherent in scaling down national or state-mandated interventions to local levels, as well as scaling up locally successful interventions to a larger region.

Interventions can also take years to make a measurable difference in water quality. Defining the temporal dimension of water quality and quantity is important in establishing the baseline and target for when the intended change is expected to take place (Hildén, 2009). The impact of a programmatic intervention or individual behavior change on water quality may not be expected to occur any time soon. In addition, the timing of the watershed management practice is important. For example, successfully establishing vegetation in a bioretention area, such as a rain garden, is dependent on the planting season and the amount of time needed for establishment of the root system.

The human dimension of water quality improvement also includes the coordination of management efforts across organizations. This involves governance issues including accountability and regulation at the individual, community, and agency (state and national) levels. An individual or small community may grapple with setting or enforcing a regulation. Multiple communities within a watershed boundary may struggle to build consensus over land use controls or commercial restrictions in an area with overlapping jurisdictions.

Linking the human and biological dimensions of conservation practices serves as a challenge to the evaluation of water quality improvement programs (Margoluis, Stem, Salafsky, & Brown, 2009). Although watershed program evaluation methods commonly include existing measures for assessing program impact, such as the physical, chemical, and biological characteristics of the land and water, meaningful evaluation that includes measures of social–contextual aspects of watershed management is needed.

Evaluation of the human dimension of water quality and quantity programs is as complex as evaluating the physical dimensions. The complexity of the causal paths of water quality problems and of interventions designed to address them is a looming issue for contextually-sensitive evaluation practice. Some water quality problems, such as the silting-up of reservoirs, are decades and possibly centuries in the making. Ameliorating the causes of silting in reservoirs requires changes in land management practices at every level within watersheds that feed reservoirs. Tilling practices of a farmer hundreds of miles from the reservoir in her watershed district impact siltage, yet she herself may never be impacted by the reservoir's loss of fishing or reduction of water capacity. The confounding externalities of the water quality problem and potential solutions to the problem present highly challenging issues for those engaged in watershed management and for the evaluation work that informs management practices.

Evaluators working within the watershed framework need to understand and address the different contextual features of this environment. Evaluators can address these contextual problems in a way that enables agencies, organizations, and community stakeholders to engage in meaningful decision making to improve water quantity and quality. The following section expands on the complexity of social-contextual considerations for water quality interventions and defines and discusses three underlying variables.

Setting Context: Social-Contextual Denominators of the Watersheds

The setting of water quality programs includes both the physical and social contexts and thus a complex and diverse array of the stakeholders. In addition, inherent in the evaluation of environmental interventions are issues of time horizons, scale, and data credibility that make it difficult to pinpoint causality, to measure impact, and to use results to influence policies and practices (Birnbaum & Mickwitz, 2009). The diversity of the biological–ecological context of specific environments such as watersheds has long been seen as an important aspect of the evaluation of those environments and of programs to preserve and protect them. This section will address three specific contextual denominators related to setting. These contextual variables apply to many environmental evaluations and relate specifically to the social dimensions of a setting context:

1. Number and diversity of stakeholder groups
2. Complexity of identifying and measuring outcomes—environmental and social
3. Differential evaluation ethos

Stakeholder Diversity

The first common denominator of the watershed setting context is the number and diversity of the stakeholders. Stakeholders are a critical part of the evaluation process. In addition, collaborations among stakeholders are important for environmental policy, especially water quality issues (Koontz & Johnson, 2004). Public policy making and implementation are increasingly handled through local, consensus-seeking collaborations involving most affected stakeholders (Leach & Pelkey, 2001; Sabatier et al., 2005). Watershed management utilizes this collaborative approach to planning, implementing, and evaluating management practices. Incorporating various stakeholder voices is important in addressing local issues, identifying those practices that negatively affect water quality and quantity, and promoting environmentally responsible behavior and practices. Specifically, water quantity and quality solutions need to incorporate the perspectives of those persons associated with the landscape and ownership of land for both agricultural and residential use (Kaplowitz & Witter, 2008). Stakeholders are critical to the process of management as well as to evaluation.

All those who live in, use, own, or manage natural resources in a watershed are stakeholders. Federal regulatory agencies, state water quality programs, county university extension agents, local landowners and land users, businesses, trade organizations, and local and national advocacy groups are stakeholders. All are involved in considering the use and effectiveness of water quality improvement practices within a watershed.

Stakeholders in many watersheds have formed collaborations or partnerships that include the diversity of ideologies and interests in the watershed; these interests include government interests as well (Born & Genskow, 2000; Koontz et al., 2004). Stakeholders are not a homogeneous group like an advocacy group that shares a common vision. Individual stakeholders hold very different beliefs, perspectives, values, and assumptions about the land, the role of government, and ways to conserve and protect water, and these beliefs and values often conflict with those of other stakeholders. For example, within a watershed working group, there may be conflict regarding the relative importance of environmental quality versus development and economic growth, or regarding the value of government regulations versus property rights. Social inequality factors further complicate the issue. Some stakeholders may have more social capital (Mullen & Allison, 1999) or economic resources than others (Morton & Padgitt, 2005). There are critical power differentials between the federal agency personnel and the local farmer, between the university-based extension agent and the city manager, between the mine owner and the commercial fisherman (Koontz et al., 2004). The perspectives of the rancher who has to haul water during the summers to his cattle are often not the same as those of the urban dweller who likes camping and hiking on weekends.

The work of watershed collaborative efforts is often both emotionally charged and highly technical (Koontz et al., 2004; Leach & Pelkey, 2001; Sabatier et al., 2005). These authors believe that expertise on social, economic, biological, and geomorphological processes is important for water conservation planning; however, they also contend that communication and consensus building can be especially difficult in a watershed because of the presence of both lay people and technical experts who often lack a common vocabulary and epistemology. It is difficult to engage diverse groups in the public discussions and decisions that are a critical part of the watershed work. Adding the vocabulary, values, and practices of evaluation to these public discussions may hinder rather than facilitate the development of strong evaluations, usable findings, and an evaluation mindset in the working group. Therefore, to promote collaboration and engagement, evaluators should utilize interactions that de-emphasize the technical vocabulary of evaluation and an "outside expert" model of communication.

Identifying and Measuring Outcomes

The complexity of identifying and measuring outcomes is a second common denominator in the setting context of watershed work. Physical indicators, such as sedimentation, nutrient levels, soil conditions, and phosphorous levels, are generally accepted targets for water quality planning but present complications for program impact evaluation. Standards are set by government agencies and are used to determine water quality. Although not without controversy, the use of physical indicators is generally accepted as the unit of analysis for watershed program evaluation. Similarly, assessing and evaluating the biophysical indicators of water quality includes measuring specific chemical and biological pollutants, stream morphology, and streambed conditions. These indicators, too, are traditional and acceptable measures of water quality. However, the complex social context of a watershed, essential in planning and evaluating water conservation practices, has been less stringently studied.

The broader environmental setting in which water quality programs are evaluated also includes the social, political, and interactional contexts that greatly impact planning and evaluating water quality improvement practices. These additional setting contexts suggest that other measures of the impact of water quality practices should be considered. In a field where physical and biophysical measures are the traditional and acceptable indicators of water quality, addressing and evaluating social and human-dimension outcomes related to water quality presents new challenges to evaluators. These social and behavioral indicators include community capacity, economic conditions and employment, education and knowledge, and behaviors such as community interactions and property and land use. Attitudes are also important social indicators. For example, there are varying attitudes and beliefs about land stewardship and ownership, locus of responsibility of problems, and larger water and climate issues.

The use of relevant primary social data, called *social indicators*, for natural resource management is gradually increasing. Social indicators are statistics and other measures that enable assessment of the social trends and the human dimensions of programs and program impacts. Not surprisingly, conflicts of goals, values, and perceptions of stakeholders complicate agreement on the definitions, importance, and use of social indicators. In addition, because the tools and history of watershed assessment are based on the physical context, consideration of social context issues may be beyond the experience, expertise, and even mindset of most stakeholders involved in the process.

Differential Evaluation Ethos

The final common denominator of the setting context is an evaluation ethos that crosses jurisdictions, geographic barriers, and stakeholder groups. Evaluation ethos includes appreciation of the importance of evaluation in decision-making, willingness to cooperate in data collection, evaluation capacity, and utilization of evaluation results. Watershed stakeholders often pursue multiple activities over a span of years to address an array of environmental issues. Stakeholders are interested in knowing whether the items and effort they invest in collaboration are likely to produce tangible results (Koontz et al., 2004; Leach & Pelkey, 2001). Some stakeholders, such as government regulatory agencies, require data gathering and value evaluation. However, other stakeholders may not appreciate evaluation or cooperate with data collection or use the results of evaluations. Although evaluations of watershed improvement projects help those involved in the initiatives to optimize their choice of interventions and use of resources, stakeholder buy in to the process is often tenuous. Those involved in BMPs often do not agree with the purpose, measures, or results of the evaluation of their practices.

Just as stakeholders are not a homogeneous group, neither are their definitions of success. There are practical and conceptual challenges of systematically measuring multiple dimensions of success for multiple stakeholders (Leach & Pelkey, 2001). Margerum (1999) suggests that evaluation of operational success for watershed-based projects is based on quantitative and qualitative assessments of outputs (e.g., plans, projects, and policies) and intangible outcomes (e.g., trust, networks, mutual understanding, and alliances). Evaluation plans must include collecting data that are relevant and credible to all stakeholders. However, because of the traditional use of physical measures of success of water quality projects, the use of social indicators may not easily be understood or have credibility with some stakeholders. Despite this lack of understanding or belief in the utility of using social indicators of success, social measures are important in understanding the impact of water quality projects.

Evaluators and planners must also work together to build local evaluation capacity. Empowering local stakeholders to think and act evaluatively about their local water and land management practices must address issues of relevance and utilization and can provide more immediate feedback for behavioral change. All involved must understand the complex change processes involved in improving, remediating, or protecting water quality.

Building capacity to create and implement plans at local and state levels, and providing data for decision-making and management practices, is crucial to the sustainability of watershed improvement programs.

The Need for Social Indicators in Environmental Evaluation

Social indicators are an important component of a framework for managing watershed protection and restoration and evaluating the impacts of watershed management practices. Pullin and Knight (2009) noted that measuring human behavior will increase in importance as interventions for environmental management become more complex. Social aspects of watershed improvement programs must be understood by evaluators in order to designate replicable successful practices and to provide accountability. But, because of the traditional use of physical indicators only, consideration of social indicators may be beyond the conceptual experience of some stakeholders.

A team at Kansas State University was able to develop the capacity of local stakeholders to understand social indicators with the use of case scenarios. Stakeholders easily identified biophysical indicators of success, but the team was unable to elicit ideas about possible social indicators of success. The team created scenarios related to the work being done by the local stakeholders. Scenarios, typically descriptions of a series of events or actions, have been used in the fields of business, computing, education, medicine, and technology to plan for or analyze future conditions, examine policy changes, as well as for the purposes of exemplifying ethical considerations. Scenarios are also used in environmental research to forecast long-range planning and policy consideration (Pulver & VanDeveer, 2009). For the evaluation team's purposes, scenarios were created to provide watershed stakeholders the context for which social indicators may be useful to measure short-term, intermediate, and long-term impacts of the BMPs in their watershed. These scenarios proved useful in facilitating thinking about the meaning of social indicators and eliciting examples of relevant social indicators of success in each example. The evaluation team was able to provide the examples to stakeholders for the purpose of developing evaluation awareness among the local group.

An Example: Social Indicators for Water Quality Management and Evaluation

The work for the Great Lakes Regional Water Program (GLRWP) illustrates how social indicators can be used in this complex environment. This initiative involved an interorganizational team drawn from USEPA, state environmental agencies, land grant universities in the upper Midwest, and others. The team developed a framework for tracking indicators of individual change, such as knowledge, awareness, capacity, constraints, and behavior. These are particularly relevant for water quality impacts from diffuse activities across the landscape. The system is now in use by state agencies and local organizations receiving program funds. Issues of data credibility, evaluation capacity, and evaluation use have been addressed by this long-term project.

GLRWP is a multistate project designed to incorporate social data into evaluation and decision making for managing water quality impacts. The initiative grew from a need for accountability and desire for improvement associated with a Clean Water Act program administered by USEPA. Although not an evaluation per se, the social indicators initiative focused on developing capacity among federal, state, and local partners to evaluate their interrelated programs and local projects (see Genskow & Prokopy, 2010). With the use of the GLRWP example, we explore the five aspects of context included in Rog's model and their application to evaluation of water quality issues. The three social-contextual denominators of the watershed landscape are a foundation for the consideration of each of Rog's contextual dimensions.

Context of the phenomenon. The context of the watershed approach to water quality issues has been discussed earlier. This specific project related to negative impacts on water quality from different water quality pollution activities in the Great Lakes Region. Scientific research and modeling have identified many aspects of the problem, but new insights continue to emerge, especially about causal relationships between landscape activities and water quality. Extensive research has analyzed and documented the various sources of these different water quality contributions nationally (Duriancik et al., 2008; USEPA, 2009; U.S. Geological Survey [USGS], 2010); however, each watershed is different and many lack detailed analysis of their specific situation. A further complication is differing standards for success across individual water restoration and protection efforts. Some focus on water quality, some on habitat or species counts, and others on practices installed by landowners or other measures.

Those conducting water quality restoration and protection projects are generally local or nongovernmental organizations (*local watershed projects* for purposes of this discussion) funded through public and private grants. They generally have some capacity to monitor water quality (and related environmental indicators) and to document funded activities (administrative reporting indicators), but very little capacity to measure, monitor, or report social data related to their programs. It is rare for watershed projects to document broader cumulative ecosystem services or aggregate impacts of program efforts.

One of the important programs addressing diffuse sources of water quality pollution is the 319 Program—a federal–state partnership administered by USEPA through authority in Section 319 of the Clean Water Act. Created through the 1987 amendments, this 319 Program provides funding to state water quality agencies specifically to address different pollution sources through voluntary approaches. It is intended to support and complement other federal, state, and local initiatives and in many respects serves as a mechanism for coordination across states.

Context of the intervention. The Great Lakes social indicators initiative illustrates an effort to build capacity among participants and partners in the 319 Program to evaluate and improve their interventions at multiple levels. The initiative (and the program interventions it seeks to influence) occurs in the context of a relatively mature program with well-established relationships across levels but including many complexities and implementation challenges. The programs are complex in terms of relationships between USEPA, state agencies, and organizations leading local watershed projects. Implementation challenges include complex causal linkages associated with the water quality phenomenon as well as the programs' reliance on voluntary action by those contributing to the water quality problems.

As part of the 319 Program, states develop protocols for assessing the nature and extent of the water quality impacts and provide funds to local watershed projects through competitive grants programs. States are expected to evaluate their overall programs, the approaches they support (voluntary technical support and incentive activities), and the local watershed projects they fund. State evaluation requirements may include using standardized reporting systems to document water quality and administrative data. Historically, there have not been consistent expectations for monitoring or reporting data about social factors—those factors likely influencing behavior change. Capacity for evaluation varies across state and local project levels.

One significant complication for evaluating program effects is the complexity of the causal mechanisms associated with poor water quality in any one place and a high likelihood of disagreement among stakeholders about local cause and appropriate management solutions. In some cases, stopping negative behaviors is a necessary but insufficient component of the problem. For example, a lake receiving nutrients from agricultural production across its watershed may have a long-term buildup of phosphorus in lake sediments that will continue to fuel water quality problems even if no new nutrients are added. Research continues to document previously unrecognized sources of contribution (such as soluble phosphorus introduced to streams through agricultural tile drains), and new technologies and practices are emerging for managing landscapes and treating nutrients (for example, biological digesters that change the form of animal waste while also harnessing energy).

The social indicators initiative began with recognition by regional program managers of the need to add formative and interim evaluative measures to learn more about steps toward success. Specifically, agency staff tapped into existing relationships with researchers at land grant universities within the region to develop new social measures. The social measures were intended to complement administrative and environmental measures already used by the program. They were also intended to be comparable across scales and over time and to be useful for program partners at local, state, and regional levels. In short, they were expected to be relevant across the multiple contexts in which local interventions were taking place. The indicators include stakeholder awareness of pollutants impairing waterways, awareness of consequences of pollutants to water quality, general water-quality related attitudes, constraints to behavior changes, and resources and technical support (Prokopy et al., 2009). A thorough discussion of the social indicators and their development process is found in Genskow and Prokopy (2010) and Prokopy et al. (2009).

Context within the broader environment (setting). As noted, the broader environment in which water quality restoration is situated includes a complex array of stakeholders, physical problems, and institutional settings. Understanding the context for individual watersheds and also state-level programs is critical for effective planning and evaluation for this issue. Determining which activities to address and where to focus efforts requires understanding the physical and social setting for interventions.

It is helpful to understand the functions of local watershed projects in these water quality efforts. Local watershed projects are local agencies or nongovernmental organizations that receive funds from state water quality agencies to conduct watershed-level programs aimed to improve water quality. Staff conducting local activities generally have training and technical expertise in applied biological and physical sciences; they are expected to work with landowners to design and install appropriate management practices consistent with water quality protection. Each grant and funding source may have distinct administrative and evaluation requirements for local managers, who may have limited resources and capacity for meeting requirements.

Depending on the setting, there may be explicit concerns that unregulated agricultural activities are not doing their fair share to resolve water quality problems. Recommended actions for reducing water quality impacts impose costs. Some of the recommendations for management practices would remove land from agricultural production (for example, leaving a strip of land along rivers or streams), introduce additional management steps (for example, soil testing before determining nutrient application), or require using land for slowing and holding (or infiltrating) water flows during storm events.

When considering appropriate evaluation approaches, it is equally important to understand the functions and influences of the state-level water quality agencies and stakeholders. Water quality programs reflect and share the same state–federal tensions as other public policy arenas. The federal Clean Water Act requires states to conduct programs to address these water quality challenges and authorizes USEPA to provide grants to states for that purpose. USEPA works with the state agencies to ensure program elements are adequate and sufficiently implemented. States are generally dependent on federal funding to conduct their programs, but many also devote substantial state resources in related efforts. Although the agencies recognize the importance of evaluation for improvement and accountability, they may resist additional federal requirements. Beyond different sources of water quality impairment, state agencies are also addressing a comprehensive array of other water resource issues (invasive species, water availability, dam safety, wetland protection, etc.). A variety of state-level interest groups interact with the state and federal agencies and legislatures about these issues, including environmental, municipal, agricultural, and professional organizations.

One additional influence of the setting on evaluation design is the importance of targeting interventions based on geography and audience characteristics. The nature of the water quality problem and its solution depend on the topography, hydrology, soil types, and land-management practices of each watershed. Some areas have threatened or impaired water quality because of those complicated relationships; other areas have very good water quality and limited immediate threats. At the state level this translates into the need to focus resources toward certain watersheds; at the local level it means understanding the variation within problematic watersheds. Even within the poor water quality areas, the impacts may be due primarily to a limited set of activities on a relatively small percentage of the land area. In those cases, evaluation would not apply to a random sample of landowners (or even agricultural producers) across a watershed. Quality information would come from an intentional selection of landowners.

Context of the evaluation. Evaluation resources and capacity are limited and variable across watershed projects. As noted, this example focuses on building capacity for evaluation of water quality programs, across local and state levels. The context for evaluation of those programs is varied, but consistently underfunded and with limited internal capacity. Resource managers may rely on modeling anticipated effects rather than measuring physical parameters. Consistent baseline and trend data are likely absent or insufficient to demonstrate attributable physical change. Data about target audiences' problem awareness or their use and awareness of potential actions to reduce impacts are generally not available.

Based on input from stakeholders (including participants testing the system), the social indicators initiative assumed there would be limited resources available for all aspects of evaluation. The effort emphasized adding capacity to use relevant social data and data-collection protocols that would add relatively little cost and would complement and help synthesize historical data collection and reporting by funded projects. The nature of the problem has made it infeasible for programs and local funders to provide answers and actionable data in short time frames. Social indicators were expected to provide interim measures that would be sensitive to showing progress

NEW DIRECTIONS FOR EVALUATION • DOI: 10.1002/ev

before physical measures could demonstrate improved water quality. The focus was on providing information about individual local watershed projects that could help establish whether they were on the right track.

Recognizing different needs across programs, the social indicators initiative developed an approach for generating relevant primary social data that provided consistency across watershed projects while also accommodating specific water quality issues, terminology, and locally appropriate practices. This was possible by using flexible but consistent questionnaires that staff in local projects could develop and manage through a common on-line tool. Although still involving time and costs associated with data collection and analysis, the use of a standardized but flexible approach minimized time requirements and implementation costs. The use of tested designs and protocols ensured an acceptable level of rigor.

In addition to complications related to time lags and scale problems, another important challenge for context in water quality evaluations involves protecting the privacy of program participants. These are largely voluntary programs. Although the need to shield participants' identities and protect private information is clearly not unique, it is complicated by the need to examine information about specific places and properties. Because the biophysical sources of the water quality problem are not uniformly distributed, their solution requires working with specific people who make decisions about specific lands. Once those places are identified on a map, that landowner is subject to potential exposure. Disclosing information about those individuals, matched to specific properties, may conflict with privacy requirements of governmental agencies and human-subjects protections required by universities or nongovernmental organizations.

Context for decision making. Typical of complex environmental management issues, there are multiple decision makers for these evaluations, and they function at multiple levels with differing expectations and influences. These include elected officials and agency staff at local, state, and federal levels. Decision-making positions are dynamic, given the long-term nature and duration of the programs and problem. Turnover occurs across elected officials and agency staff and leadership positions. All of those changes can influence specific expectations for rigor and emphasis.

As noted, local watershed projects are components of local organizations and agencies that obtain grants from multiple sources. They also answer to multiple decision makers including their own boards, constituents, or local elected officials. Beyond wanting to improve and protect water quality, those decision makers are interested in broader economic and multiplier benefits associated with the activities and outcomes. They also need to satisfy local stakeholders and justify continued or expanded funding from multiple sources. Highly visible indicators such as midsummer algal blooms or contaminated wells can increase public dissatisfaction and calls for action.

Decision makers at state- and federal-level agencies and legislatures focus on whether the right actions were taken, how practices have changed, whether water quality improved, and how well funds are spent. They are also interested in exploring alternative approaches and understanding limitations associated with individual programs. Organized interests keep attention focused on the perceived fairness of various approaches (regulated versus voluntary) and look to evaluations of water quality programs as evidence for their positions. Ultimately, at the federal level, decision makers want to know how programs advance the goals of the Clean Water Act and related legislation to protect and restore water quality.

Summary. This example illustrates the complexity of evaluating voluntary water quality programs and the importance of context at all levels. An evaluation of a national, regional, or state program that ignores the nuances of context in selecting appropriate methodological approaches would miss the mark. Focusing solely on documented water quality improvements (whether or not they can be causally linked to program interventions) ignores much of the actual focus of these water quality projects (voluntary use of appropriate management practices in the correct places). Randomized designs ignoring contextual dimensions such as the critical contributions of specific places and landowner practices to specific problems provide little benefit for understanding improvements to water quality. The complexities of scale, time lags, resources, decision makers, and the nature of the problem itself reinforce the importance of understanding context and emphasizing evaluation as an opportunity for program correction or improvement.

Conclusions and Recommendations for Evaluation of Water Quality Interventions

Evaluation is an integral component of water quality improvement. The evaluation of quality improvement initiatives at the watershed level is useful for several reasons. Such evaluations assist in identifying and dealing with issues as they arise from the project, monitoring the impact of local projects, comparing local projects to draw lessons, and collecting detailed information as part of larger state- or region-wide water quality evaluations. Evaluations of small-scale quality improvement projects help those involved in the initiatives to optimize their choice of interventions and use of resources. Evaluations of small-scale and large-scale projects can inform policy as well as practice.

Many questions can be raised about the water quality improvement programs. Do they work? How can they be improved? What factors promote or inhibit their success? What can we learn from local experiences? How can stakeholder buy-in be facilitated? How can individuals be motivated to use BMPs? Evaluation can help answer the many questions related to conserving, preserving, and protecting our nation's water resources.

The broad and unique challenges involved in evaluating water quality programs require that evaluators utilize contextually sensitive evaluation practices. In the watershed setting, these practices should involve understanding the relationship of evaluation of watershed management practices to water quality and quantity, establishing stakeholder buy-in for program evaluation, defining and measuring both physical and social indicators of program success and utilizing appropriate evaluation designs, building evaluation capacity of local stakeholders, and collaborating with stakeholders to develop a systematic cultural change within the water quality community to adopting an evaluation ethos. These can all be described within Rog's contextual dimensions for evaluation, with specific importance lent to the social context and the interaction of the physical and the social aspects of the watershed environment. The GLRWP social indicators initiative example demonstrates the practical aspects of such consideration.

Building capacity at local and state levels, and providing data for decision making and management practices, is crucial to the sustainability of watershed improvement programs. In particular, the biological and social aspects of watershed improvement programs must be understood to replicate successful practices and provide accountability to stakeholders. The need to design and test an evaluation framework that will enable stakeholders to document and report on the contributions of watershed improvement programs is vital to achieving this goal.

References

Birnbaum, M., & Mickwitz, P. (2009). Editors' notes. In M. Birnbaum & P. Mickwitz (Eds.), *Environmental program and policy evaluation: Addressing methodological challenges. New Directions for Evaluation, 122,* 1–7.

Born, S. M., & Genskow, K. D. (2000). *The watershed approach: An empirical assessment of innovation in environmental management.* Washington, DC: National Academy of Public Administration.

Bruyninckx, H. (2009). Environmental evaluation practices and the issue of scale. In M. Birnbaum & P. Mickwitz (Eds.), *Environmental program and policy evaluation: Addressing methodological challenges. New Directions for Evaluation, 122,* 31–39.

Duriancik, L. F., Bucks, D., Dobrowolski, J. P., Drewes, T., Eckles, S. D., Jolly, L., . . . Weltz, M. A. (2008). The first five years of the Conservation Effects Assessment Project. *Journal of Soil and Water Conservation, 63,*185A–197A.

Genskow, K., & Prokopy, L. (2010). Lessons learned in developing social indicators for regional water quality management. *Society and Natural Resources, 23,* 83–91.

Hildén, M. (2009). Time horizons in evaluating environmental policies. In M. Birnbaum & P. Mickwitz (Eds.), *Environmental program and policy evaluation: Addressing methodological challenges. New Directions for Evaluation, 122,* 9–18.

Hooper, B. P., McDonald, G. T., & Mitchell, B. (1999). Facilitating integrated resource and environmental management: Australian and Canadian perspectives. *Journal of Environmental Planning and Management, 42,* 747–766.

Kaplowitz, M., & Witter, S. (2008). Agricultural and residential stakeholder input for watershed management in a mid-Michigan watershed. *Landscape and Urban Planning, 84,* 20–27.

Koontz, T. M., & Johnson, E. M. (2004). One size does not fit all: Matching breadth of stakeholder participation to watershed group accomplishments. *Policy Sciences, 37,* 185–204.

Koontz, T. M., Steelman, T. A., Carmin, J., Korfmacher, K. S., Mosely, C., & Thomas, C. W. (2004). *Collaborative environmental management: What roles for government?* Washington, DC: Resources for the Future.

Leach, W. D., & Pelkey, N. W. (2001). Making watershed partnerships work: A review of the empirical literature. *Journal of Water Resources Planning and Management, 127,* 378–385.

Margerum, R. D. (1999). Integrated environmental management: The foundations for successful practice. *Environmental Management, 24*(2), 151–166.

Margoluis, R., Stem, C., Salafsky, N., & Brown, M. (2009). Design alternatives for evaluating the impact of conservation projects. In M. Birnbaum & P. Mickwitz (Eds.), *Environmental program and policy evaluation: Addressing methodological challenges. New Directions for Evaluation, 122,* 85–96.

Morton, L. W., & Padgitt, S. (2005). Selecting socio-economic metrics for watershed management. *Environmental Monitoring and Assessment, 103,* 83–98.

Mullen, M. W., & Allison, B. (1999). Stakeholder involvement and social capital: Keys to watershed management success in Alabama. *Journal of the American Water Resources Association, 35,* 655–662.

Prokopy, L., Genskow, K., Asher, J., Baumgart-Getz, A., Bonnell, J., Broussard, S., . . . Wood, D. (2009). Designing a regional system of social indicators to evaluate nonpoint source water projects. *Journal of Extension, 47.*

Pullin, A. S., & Knight, T. M. (2009). Data credibility: A perspective from systematic reviews in environmental management. In M. Birnbaum & P. Mickwitz (Eds.), *Environmental program and policy evaluation: Addressing methodological challenges. New Directions for Evaluation, 122,* 65–74.

Pulver, S., & VanDeveer, S. D. (2009). "Thinking about tomorrows": Scenarios, global environmental politics, and social science scholarship. *Global Environmental Politics, 9,* 1–13.

Rog, D. (2012). When background becomes foreground: Toward context-sensitive evaluation practice. In D. J. Rog, J. L. Fitzpatrick, & R. F. Conner (Eds.), *Context: A framework for its influence on evaluation practice. New Directions for Evaluation, 135,* pp. 25–40.

Sabatier, P. A., Focht, W., Lubell, M., Trachtenberg, Z., Vedlitz, A., & Matlock, M. (Eds.). (2005). *Swimming upstream: Collaborative approaches to watershed management.* Cambridge, MA: MIT Press.

U.S. Environmental Protection Agency (USEPA). (2009). *National water quality inventory: Report to Congress, 2004 reporting cycle* (Publication EPA 841-R-08–001). Washington, DC: USEPA.

USEPA. (1996). *Watershed approach framework.* Retrieved from http://water.epa.gov/type/watersheds/framework.cfm

U.S. Geological Survey (USGS). (2010). *The quality of our nation's waters—Nutrients in the nation's streams and groundwater, 1992–2004* (USGS Circular 1350). Washington, DC: U.S. Department of the Interior.

Wood, C. (2008). *Dry spring: The coming water crisis of North America.* Berkeley, CA: Raincoast Books.

LINDA P. THURSTON is assistant dean of the College of Education and Professor of Special Education, Counseling and Student Affairs at Kansas State University (KSU). She founded the Office of Educational Innovation and Evaluation at KSU and recently served as a program officer at the National Science Foundation, working with broadening participation and evaluation programs.

CHRISTA A. SMITH is a research associate and evaluator at the Office of Educational Innovation and Evaluation (OEIE) at Kansas State University in Manhattan, Kansas. OEIE provides comprehensive and collaborative project development, strategic planning, and evaluation services for local, national, and international projects.

KENNETH GENSKOW is an assistant professor of environmental planning in the Department of Urban and Regional Planning at University of Wisconsin–Madison (UW) and serves as a water resources specialist with UW Cooperative Extension. His work addresses human dimensions of natural resources and environmental management, including evaluation of outreach and technical assistance approaches.

LINDA STALKER PROKOPY is an associate professor of natural resources planning at Purdue University. Her research, teaching, and extension all focus on the human dimensions of natural resources, with an emphasis on watershed management. She is especially interested in understanding how to use education and outreach to inform behavior change.

WILLIAM L. HARGROVE is the director of the Center for Environmental Research and Management. He is also a professor emeritus of Kansas State University where he was the director of the Kansas Center for Agricultural Resources and the Environment.

NEW DIRECTIONS FOR EVALUATION • DOI: 10.1002/ev

LaFrance, J., Nichols, R., & Kirkhart, K. E. (2012). Culture writes the script: On the centrality of context in indigenous evaluation. In D. J. Rog, J. L. Fitzpatrick, & R. F. Conner (Eds.), *Context: A framework for its influence on evaluation practice. New Directions for Evaluation, 135*, 59–74.

4

Culture Writes the Script: On the Centrality of Context in Indigenous Evaluation

Joan LaFrance, Richard Nichols, Karen E. Kirkhart

Abstract

Context grounds all aspects of indigenous evaluation. From an indigenous evaluation framework (IEF), programs are understood within their relationship to place, setting, and community, and evaluations are planned, undertaken, and validated in relation to cultural context. This chapter describes and explains fundamental elements of IEF epistemology and method and gives several examples of these elements from evaluations in American Indian communities. IEF underscores the importance of putting context ahead of method choice and suggests that context exerts an even greater impact than previously recognized. © Wiley Periodicals, Inc., and the American Evaluation Association.

In proposing her unified theory of context in evaluation, Rog (2009) defined five aspects of context: problem context, intervention context, setting, evaluation context, and decision-making context. She located culture as one of six dimensions within each aspect. This chapter uses the example of an indigenous evaluation framework (IEF) to illustrate the centrality of context to one's evaluation approach or methodology. In so doing, we argue that culture plays an even larger role than Rog has envisioned. IEF demonstrates how culture infuses all contexts and defines methodology itself; it is not simply one of several descriptive but separate dimensions that could be included or omitted, considered or not considered. One cannot step outside cultural context in practicing evaluation. Although considerations of culture must never be ignored, particular cultural identifications (e.g., ethnicity, nationality, community affiliation, language, social class, age, health status, disability, immigration history, gender, sexual orientation) may be more or less salient within a given evaluation context. Rog posits the five aspects of context working together, so careful examination of the problem context, the program context, the setting, and the decision-making context sheds further light on these salient cultural intersections. Rog's intent is to get to actionable evidence. To do so requires attention to epistemology, which sets the parameters of legitimate knowledge and is itself culturally defined.

The IEF was developed in response to requests from tribal colleges to have an evaluation model that would be more respectful of their settings than Western models imposed by external funding organizations. With support from the National Science Foundation (grant number REC-0438720) to the American Indian Higher Education Consortium, Joan LaFrance and Richard Nichols developed the model with assistance from expert advisors and focus groups and pilot tested it with tribal college personnel and Indian K–12 educators.

Bringing context from background to foreground is not new for indigenous evaluation. IEF is a framework defined by context and understood within it. Context defines the methodology of an indigenous approach, inclusive of both epistemology and method. Pragmatic concerns of budget and other resources of time, data, and capacity, while still relevant, yield to more fundamental concerns of what counts as evidence, how knowledge is gained, and what evaluation approach will benefit the community, both through what is learned during the evaluation process and through the findings or results.

The primary focus of this chapter is the context of evaluation; however, this chapter also speaks strongly to setting as a defining aspect of methodology. IEF is defined by its physical and cultural location, in a way that expands Rog's (2009) definition of setting as the "environment surrounding the intervention/program." In that definition, the focus is on intervention, the surrounding environment blurring in contrast with the sharper programmatic image. In IEF, the setting defines everything, including the understandings of what constitutes a social problem, appropriate responses to that problem, meaningful evaluation of the problem and/or the response, and useful knowledge to advance the well-being of the tribal community.

Rog begins with method choice as her focal concern; posing the question, "What methods provide the highest quality and most actionable evidence for whom in which contexts?" Her explicit intent is to push back against a "methods-first approach" (i.e., one that privileges certain methods irrespective of context) and to make more nuanced selections that are "context-sensitive." Her five aspects of context are ones that she deems important to consider "in choosing methods and in carrying out an evaluation (from design to reporting)" (Rog, 2009).

NEW DIRECTIONS FOR EVALUATION • DOI: 10.1002/ev

Indigenous evaluation takes the focal concern back to methodology, inclusive of both epistemology and method choice. IEF is a context-first approach. It is, in a sense, the epitome of context-sensitive evaluation practice, though our interpretation of this concept may extend beyond Rog's vision, as discussed below.

Overview

Indigenous evaluation is not just a matter of accommodating or adapting majority perspectives to American Indian contexts. Rather, it requires a total reconceptualization and rethinking. It involves a fundamental shift in worldview. Indigenous methodology challenges us to rethink both epistemology and method. Although methods of indigenous evaluation share common ground with qualitative methods, the two are not synonymous. Not all indigenous methodology is qualitative, nor are all qualitative methods congruent with indigenous contexts.

The fundamental elements of epistemology and method within indigenous methodology are illustrated in the work of Margaret Kovach (2010) and Vivian Jiménez Estrada (2005) as well as previously unpublished case examples of two American Indian evaluators, Carol Davis and Dawn Frank. Together, they help map tribal epistemologies and illustrate a blend of culturally specific and culturally adapted evaluation methods. Storytelling and metaphor also serve as methods to anchor indigenous evaluation to symbolic and textual references holding deep ties to the culture of a people and place.

An indigenous framework also has implications for validity. Context is critical to valid inference; programs can be accurately understood only within their relationship to place, setting, and community. Working deeply within indigenous cultures and communities simultaneously supports validity and expands validity arguments. Methodological justifications of validity such as those argued by Rog must be placed in cultural context, supported by justifications grounded in theory, life experience, interpersonal connections, and concern for social consequences. Each of these justificatory perspectives will be illustrated with indigenous examples.

Consideration of consequences bridges, in the following section of this chapter, to a brief but important discussion of issues of sovereignty and ownership of evaluation data and of the process itself. The next section reflects on the implications and limitations of the indigenous framework for evaluation practice within and outside of American Indian contexts. Depending on the evaluation question, an indigenous approach may or may not be useful even in an indigenous context. The chapter closes with reflection on Rog's model, specifically on her proposal that context be moved from background to foreground, from a character role to a leading role in our evaluations. But what if the role is cast even larger? An indigenous framing of evaluation illustrates how context in fact writes the story itself.

NEW DIRECTIONS FOR EVALUATION • DOI: 10.1002/ev

Ways of Knowing: Epistemology as Methodology

Research and evaluation are about creating knowledge. Generally, the epistemological orientations for evaluation stem either from a Western positivist paradigm that posits a neutral or objective stance toward the natural world or from a constructivist position that recognizes subjective and multiple realities. Both of these paradigms are based on Western constructions of knowing, not indigenous epistemologies. Contextualization of research and evaluation involves not only assessing and being sensitive to environment, but also examining the epistemological paradigms underlying the ways in which knowledge is viewed. Epistemologies that define the knowledge creation and axiology or values for use of knowledge are mediated by culture. Increasingly, indigenous scholars are giving voice to indigenous epistemology and defining its role in shaping their research (Estrada, 2005; Wilson, 2008; Kovach, 2010; Weber-Pillwax, 1999). Cree scholar Margaret Kovach (2010) argues that indigenous methods do not come from Western philosophy but rather flow from tribal epistemologies. She recognizes that there is similarity among tribal worldviews; however, she would further contextualize indigenous epistemologies to a specific tribal situation.

An indigenous worldview embodies the notion that all things are living, spiritual entities and interrelated, including knowledge. Also, there is a profound sense of place woven throughout native thought (Basso, 1996). It is this sense of place that gives rise to a tribal culture. For example, Plains Indian culture is defined by those tribal peoples' relationship to the Plains' physical geography, its landmarks, and the stories that relate to them, as well as the creatures that inhabit those spaces. Creation stories define human life in concert with the earth and sky, which differs from a worldview common in Western culture where a supreme being is separate from nature and humans are given dominion over the material world. Tewa scholar Gregory Cajete (2000) defines models, causality, interpretation, and explanation in ways that go beyond objective measurement but honor the importance of direct experience, interconnectedness, relationship, holism, and value. He writes:

> It is the depth of our ancient human participation with nature that has been lost and indeed must be regained in some substantial form in modern life and modern science. The cosmological and philosophical must once again become "rooted" in a life-centered, lived experience of the natural world. (p. 5)

Indigenous knowledge values holistic thinking that contrasts with the linear or hierarchical thinking that characterizes much of Western evaluation practice. As Kovach argues, "knowledge is neither acultural nor apolitical" and there is a need to recognize distinctly indigenous ways of knowing that influence one's approach to doing research and by extension, evaluation (Kovach, 2010, p. 30).

Figure 4.1. Indigenous Evaluation Model

Introducing indigenous ways of knowing into evaluation practice provides a foundation for IEF. In the IEF model (see Figure 4.1) indigenous knowledge encircles the framework. It provides the foundation for understanding the world and is found in the traditions of a people, their creation stories, clan origins, and the encounters of their ancestors. It also includes empirical knowledge gained through careful observation from multiple perspectives and revealed knowledge acquired through dreams, visions, and ceremony.

Knowledge has function and, as a living entity, it has moral purpose. The late Lakota scholar Vine Deloria Jr. (1999) explained that the elders were interested in finding the proper moral and ethical road upon which humans should walk and, for knowledge to be useful, it should be directed toward that goal. Everything that humans experience has value and provides some aspect of instruction. Deloria notes that

> Absent in this approach was the idea that knowledge existed apart from human beings and their communities, and could stand alone for "its own sake." In the Indian conception, it was impossible that there could be abstract propositions that could be used to explore the structure of the physical world. Knowledge was derived from individual and communal experiences in daily

life, in keen observation of the environment, and in interpretive message they
received from spirits in ceremonies, visions and dreams. (p. 44)

The holistic framing of an indigenous worldview and the extensive
sense of interrelationship, community, and family require privileging indigenous views of the source and purposes of knowledge and situating evaluation within a sense of place and time. The notion central to empirical
methodology that one can separate out program variables for independent
analysis is neither useful nor congruent with an indigenous way of knowing. Learning and knowledge derive from experiencing the program, and it
is the subjectivity of this experience that leads to meaning and understanding. Deloria (1999) explains that the elders cautioned, "we cannot 'misex-
perience' anything; we can only misinterpret what we experience. Therefore,
in some instances we can experience something entirely new, and so we
must be alert and try not to classify things too quickly" (p. 46).

Indigenous knowledge cannot be standardized (Kovach, 2010); however, Cora Weber-Pillwax (1999), a Métis researcher, has described principles that should guide methods based on indigenous ways of knowing. The
first, based on the recognition of the interconnectedness of all living things,
is the mandate for respect, which goes beyond knowing rituals and practices and protocols. It is: "believing and living that relationship with all
forms of life, and conducting all interactions in a spirit of kindness and hon-
esty" (Weber-Pillwax, 1999, p. 41). Respecting relationship requires a motivation to contribute to the community and a belief that as an evaluator/
researcher you will benefit only to the degree that your work benefits others. She explains that the foundation of research is the lived indigenous
experience and this must ground the work, not theories or ideas that are
brought to bear on this experience. Theories will "spring from the people
themselves—theories that explain the many facets and connections of our
individual and collective lives" (Weber-Pillwax, 1999, pp. 42–43). Trans-
formation results through internalization of the learning. This assumes that
the evaluators/researchers take responsibility for transformations and take
into account the broad community interrelationships when making decisions regarding research choices. Finally, and most important for the theme
of this chapter, indigenous research is grounded in the integrity of the community. If the research methodology is right, it is right only for that community, because it is only there that it has integrity.

Indigenous epistemologies are realized through their expressions in
specific, grounded tribal epistemologies. Kovach (2010) describes Nêhiýaw
Kiskêýihtamowin (Plains Cree knowledges) that includes a tribal-based
holistic epistemology, story, purpose, experience, ethics, ways of gaining
knowledge, and a consideration of the historical colonial relationships of her
people. Vivian Jiménez Estrada (2005) draws from her Maya culture to describe
the Ceiba, The Tree of Life. Using this cultural metaphor, she examines how it

defines research methodology within an indigenous context. She finds direction through the representations of each element of the tree: the bark that provides structure to ensure values respecting time and place are respected, the trunk with its life-promoting energies that respect the ideologies with which she allies her research, and the branches that inform the responsibility to "share the protocols with the respect and reverence that not only participants deserve, but life itself" (p. 50).

Dawn Frank (2010) describes how the Lakota concepts of *Mitakuye Oyasin* (all my relations) and *wolakokiciyapi* (learning Lakota ways of life in community) influenced the development of her research methodology. A three-dimensional braided model represents elements of Lakota ways of knowing and respect and elements of Western scientific inquiry. She explains how, after being assimilated into Western science culture to develop a researchable hypothesis for her dissertation, she had to return to her Lakota roots to reevaluate the research and then develop a model and methodology that considered Lakota laws and protocols.

In an NSF-funded program led by Dr. Carol Davis (Turtle Mountain Chippewa), the North Dakota Tribal College Faculty, in collaboration with the North Dakota University Faculty and the North Dakota Association of Tribal Colleges, developed a context-specific model for guiding undergraduate student research in science (Davis, Long Feather, & Padmanabhan, 2007). The process of building students' knowledge and skills is grounded in an inclusive circular model of mentoring students that recognizes the influence of family and community as well as faculty members within the Tribal College and the University. Research results are scrutinized in terms of their value to the community, their relationship to traditional cultural knowledge, and their impact on community members now and into the future, out to the seventh generation. The possibility of harm is considered alongside concerns of reliability and validity. Sharing of research includes culturally appropriate presentation of information, with specific attention to relationships that need to be addressed in reporting, including use of ceremony, approval of elders, and discussions with community. The sharing stage is also seen as an opportunity to inquire and explore new research, honoring the cyclical nature of research and evaluation under this model.

These examples illustrate that indigenous epistemologies share common understandings while also being shaped into culturally and tribally specific methodological models. The IEF acknowledges that we need to privilege our own epistemologies. It defines general characteristics of these epistemologies without claiming to define one standard. Rather, the framework suggests that those who want to apply an indigenous approach to research or evaluation consult tribal cultural experts to understand tribal ways of knowing for that community. This process is often implicit. It can be brought to life through language, protocols for behaving, deeply held relationships within the community and with the land, and the people's lived experiences.

Values and Methodology

In the IEF model, indigenous knowledge forms a circle around core values. The axiology of indigenous research and evaluation is connected to epistemological notions of relationship. Values become central to methodology based on relationship or what Opaskwayak Cree scholar Shawn Wilson (2008) describes as *relational accountability*. "In essence this means that the methodology needs to be based in a community context (be relational) and has to demonstrate respect, reciprocity and responsibility (be accountable as it is put into action)" (p. 99). In the IEF, the core values of place, community, honoring individual gifts, and sovereignty inform an evaluation methodology that reinforces the relationship and responsibility to land, community, individuals, and nationhood.

Honoring a sense of place requires evaluation to fit within the contours of the location, including its history and contemporary realities. Honoring community requires transparent methods that embrace inclusion and participation. Honoring the gifts of each individual necessitates respectful assessments of performance and progress. Ross (1992) describes how he came to understand this value from Canadian aboriginal elders:

> The duty of all people, therefore, is to assist others on their paths, and to be patient when their acts or words demonstrate that there are things still to be learned. The corollary duty is to avoid discouraging people by belittling them in any fashion and so reducing their respect for and faith in themselves. (p. 27)

Finally, honoring sovereignty recognizes nationhood. It reaffirms place, community, culture, language, and political presence. Indigenous evaluation methodology is explicitly related to nation building (Robertson, Jorgenson, & Garrow, 2004). It seeks to contribute to the health and well-being of the community first and foremost rather than to generalization to larger audiences or other settings.

Although these values resonate in most tribal communities, the IEF does not suggest that they are the only values or the defining values that influence indigenous evaluation. As with tribal-specific epistemologies, the values that guide research and evaluation methods need to be defined at the tribal level and are understood through a community's traditional knowledge, lived experience, and spiritual expressions.

Story as Metaphor and Method

Telling stories is fundamental to being indigenous peoples. Stories are a method and means for understanding the consequences of lived experience. Indigenous evaluation is about telling stories. Stories can employ lexical form as well as visual symbols or metaphors, song, and prayer. Both the story and related metaphors are culturally nuanced and contextually situated

(Kovach, 2010). Aware of the power of metaphor and story, the authors of the IEF sought ways to use them to explain evaluation from an indigenous perspective. Eric Jolly, one of the advisors for the project, provided both the metaphor and story for the IEF by sharing what he had been taught by his grandmother while learning to weave a Cherokee basket. He explained that the basket-making process begins by interweaving two pairs of thin honey-suckle vines into a square or cross that forms the base of the basket and which symbolizes the four directions and elements of creation. On the journey of life, this represents the beginning of spiritual awareness. Additional pairs of vines are woven together, and with the original crossed sets of vines, they begin to form interwoven triangles that give shape to the basket. The inter-connection symbolizes the spiritual relationships of the creator with human-ity, animals, and all that is on earth. As the weaving continues, there are sets of concentric circles that form inner and outer walls that are held in tension, giving the basket its strength. It is this strength that gives the basket its integrity, for a strong basket is a useful basket. Also, as the basket is being woven, it is continuously turned to ensure that it forms a balanced whole.

The story of the Cherokee basket became a metaphor for the relation-ship of indigenous evaluation to program implementation: Each is inter-laced with the other. Evaluation requires this continuous reflection and learning to ensure that multiple perspectives are included in the interpre-tation of the program experience (LaFrance & Nichols, 2009).

The IEF invites the creation of culturally rooted metaphors as a way to begin the process of story creation. Metaphor replaces the Western concept of the logic model, which is based on a linear and a causal relationship between actions and outcomes. The metaphors created with the use of the IEF do not necessarily have to represent a causal model, but they symboli-cally represent images that have meaning within the cultural context of the program and its evaluation. The following are examples of program metaphors, developed by four different tribal college personnel using IEF.

An Ojibwe group from the Great Lakes used a canoe as the metaphor for a program that had a goal of building an environmental science cur-riculum based on the 13 moons of the Ojibwe calendar. Thirteen moons surrounding a canoe represented the seasonal content of the curriculum for each month. Various elements of the canoe represented cultural values guid-ing the curriculum philosophy based on the wisdom of elders and the seven teachings of the Ojibwe, and the roles of elders and youth. The image cap-tured the relationship of elders and youth, traditional values and curricu-lum philosophy and content, which are all the elements of the program. It also illustrated the relationship of the program (the canoe) with evaluation (the oars), and it is the oars that guide the navigation of the program.

In another example, a Plains tribe's Winter Count—a buffalo hide cal-endar with pictures or symbols depicting memorable events—was used as the metaphor for a comprehensive project to introduce students to science, nurs-ing, and mathematics. Among tribes of the Great Plains, the Winter Count was used to record important events over the course of a year, from first snowfall to next first snowfall. The group used this metaphor to represent key relationships and activities of the program. These included environmental restoration, engaging youth with elders, and using the outdoors as classrooms.

A group from a desert tribe drew a mural as their metaphor for their bridging program, which prepares students for employment or enrollment in the tribal college's transfer program. The mural represented various pathways for students to take and the program resources (such as child care, transportation, and financial aid) to support their journeys. In the history of this tribe, journeys were made from the desert to the ocean to collect salt, which is considered a powerful medicine. Success in the program is represented by salt needed all along the journey. Thus, the word *salt* appeared several times along the various program pathways as it represented the spiritual sustenance needed by each student to successfully complete the journey.

A Pacific Northwest tribal group used the metaphor of a cedar tree for their program, a first-year experience that is a set of interdisciplinary courses for those just entering college. The cedar tree is used in tribal ceremonies and has great cultural significance and meaning. The roots of the tree represented the traditions and language of the people. The trunk of the tree was the program with its strength representing building trust, strengthening school–community relationships, and changing pedagogical practices. Various branches of the tree reflected program elements of the first-year experience, including learning communities, place-based learning activities, engaged faculty, and co-curricular activities. The image illustrated core tribal values that at this tribal college are reflected in respect for the teaching of the ancestors and elders, care of the community and the land, and respect for culture and language. Finally, the upper portion of the trunk was the program evaluation.

These examples illustrate the power of symbols and place among tribal peoples. Use of stories has always been a means for passing on "teachings, medicines, and practices that can assist members of the collective" (Kovach, 2010, p. 95). IEF establishes metaphor as a way to create story by replacing the "proposal language" of goals, activities, outputs, and outcomes with images that have rich cultural grounding. In this way, evaluation becomes the process of telling the story and reflection on the lessons learned.

To tell the story, the IEF model proceeds to the next phase of evaluation, building the scaffolding. It describes evaluation design and processes in ways that deeply respect tribal values. Elements or plot lines are selected for examination (forming the evaluation questions), the data to be gathered and their sources are identified, timelines are established, and analysis and reporting procedures or tasks are specified. This phase is somewhat analogous to evaluation design but involves taking account of cultural and community considerations. For example, the IEF illustrates ways to shift evaluation questions, which may be seen as rude and/or intrusive from a tribal perspective, to evaluative statements. From an indigenous perspective, data-gathering tools such as interviewing, especially when dealing with tribal elders, involve taking time to build a relationship of trust, through conversation rather than quizzing for information. Furthermore, the use of cultural and/or tribal protocols becomes a matter of personal growth for the indigenous evaluator. These are matters not only to be "taken into consideration," but to be learned, practiced, and internalized, resulting in cultural reaffirmation.

The next two phases of the IEF model are planning, implementing, and celebrating evaluation; and engaging community and building capacity. These phases are also based on indigenous cultural values. Planning and executing the evaluation are inclusive processes, with the evaluator viewed as a partner in the lived experience of the program. This positioning enables ongoing reflection and learning. It also makes the process of evaluation transparent and provides opportunities for capacity building. Respect also means negotiating ownership of information and a willingness to work with tribal internal review boards or research committees (LaFrance & Crazy Bull, 2009). Often, permission to disseminate one's evaluation work products must be sought on a case-by-case basis. The dissemination of evaluation findings within the community or tribe also becomes a celebration, the culmination of a knowledge-creation process.

The tools used in doing indigenous evaluation may be similar to those used by nonindigenous evaluators. However, culture is guiding their use and may dictate the development of new tools or the use of tribally specific tools. Evaluation, as storytelling, is culturally and contextually bound, just as understanding what has merit and worth is mediated by culture and community.

To summarize, the IEF involves a fundamental paradigm shift in which the nature of knowledge itself expands beyond empirical knowledge to include traditional knowledge and revealed knowledge. It redefines culturally bound understandings of "actionable evidence" and privileges place-based, experiential knowledge as valuable to learning and improving both programs and the broader communities of which they are a part. IEF expands and enriches method, inclusive of both designs and information-gathering strategies and tools. Designs are often emergent, time frames generous. Evaluators step in rhythm with the community rather than setting their own pace. Holistic understandings of interconnectedness are valued more than the postpositivist notions of isolating variables to explore causality and generalizability. Information-gathering strategies are relational, reflecting the nature of knowledge itself. Communities may create and utilize new strategies specific to their local context or they may take fresh approaches to strategies already recognized as legitimate tools of data collection.

Culturally Contextualizing Validity

Rog's (2009) focus on context is in the service of achieving high-quality, actionable evidence. Though the language may differ, none would question the need for trustworthy information with which to guide programs or policies. Based on her professional training and extensive experience, Rog (2011) is fundamentally concerned with attaining the strongest possible inferences of causality. Accuracy of causal inference is an important and relevant validity concern, though not the only such concern, even within a traditional Campbellian typology (Chen, Donaldson, & Mark, 2011). When one moves beyond inquiry grounded in postpositivist epistemology and explores alternatives such as constructivism, critical theory, or culturally specific epistemology, the construct of validity must expand accordingly. Narrow definitions of validity constrain how scientific rigor is understood and operationalized, limiting professional legitimation of culturally based paradigms (Johnson et al., 2008). Mirroring Rosaldo's (1993) call to expand and redefine what we mean by culture, Kirkhart (2005) has argued that the construct of validity must be capacious enough to encompass work guided by both traditional and alternate paradigms. Working within IEF, indigenous epistemology calls us to rethink traditional understandings of validity and broaden the bases on which validity is argued. The five justifications of multicultural validity identified by Kirkhart (1995, 2005) can assist in that process. They are: experiential, interpersonal, methodological, consequential, and theoretical.

Indigenous evaluation does not emphasize causation as it is framed in a postpositivist epistemology; however, it does emphasize relationships with a context. Genuine understandings are grounded in place, setting, and community. Experiential justifications of validity, those grounded in the lived experiences of participants, are central to an indigenous framework. As noted above, knowledge is derived from individual and communal experience in daily life, in keen observations of the environment, and in interpretive messages received from spirits in ceremonies, visions, and dreams (Deloria, 1999). Local language may be required to capture the meaning most closely related to the English-language expression of validity. For example, Kovach (2010) writes,

> In considering research validity, I hear the Elders' voices: Are you doing this in a good way? There is a Cree word, *tâpwê*, which means to speak the truth. This is about validity or, relationally speaking, credibility. To do this means to tend to the process in a good way, so that no matter the outcome you can sleep at night because you did right by the process. (p. 52)

Doing the process in a good way involves community accountability. Validity under indigenous epistemology is holistic and relational. Interpersonal justifications are grounded in relationship, though here the person-centered terminology fails to capture the full scope of relationship to context, inclusive of animals, nature, and the cosmos. Methodological justifications here refer to measurement and design procedures that support validity arguments. In general, they are the most similar to Western arguments, but in the details, they may appear quite different. For example, Frank's (2010) methods of conducting interviews with tribal elders were grounded in three unwritten *Woope* (Lakota laws), which may be thought of as custom law, natural law, and spiritual law.

> Lakota protocol included presentation of a gift and an opportunity to pray to the creator for what was discussed in the interview and for mentioning any individuals in our discussion who may be deceased. The deceased were also honored with a tobacco offering after the interview was completed. This Lakota protocol provided comfort to the elders, knowing that their deceased relatives would be respected. (p. 58)

Interestingly, indigenous epistemology shares Rog's commitment to action; it is action oriented (Kovach, 2010). Consequential justifications of validity are therefore extremely important. Inquiry is expected to give back to the community and support tribal sovereignty and well-being. The value of the evaluation is judged in part by what it contributes to the collective good. Understandings that do not translate into community benefit may be flawed or incomplete. Theory-based justifications may draw upon characteristics of indigenous theory itself or be adapted from Western theoretical frameworks. Maori scholar Graham Smith (cited in Kovach, 2010, p. 47) describes indigenous theory as located within a culturally contextual site, born of organic process involving community, reflecting an indigenous worldview and focused on change. Examples of Western frameworks that have been adapted include: relational theory, participatory action research (Wilson, 2008), and critical theory (Kovach, 2010). When invoking Western theories in this justification, the intent is not to seek external validation, but instead to provide "a complementary framework for accepting the uniqueness of an Indigenous research paradigm" (Wilson, 2008, p. 16). To support validity, theory must be congruent with the context of practice (Kirkhart, 2010).

Our intent here is to illustrate how the terrain of validity arguments necessarily widens when reflecting on the quality of evaluation undertaken from an indigenous perspective; we do not wish to reify categories. These (and quite possibly other) justifications work singly and in combination in response to setting, to support strong, trustworthy understandings. Rather than thinking of the five justificatory perspectives of multicultural validity categorically, the image of a web (Kovach, 2010) may more accurately reflect the process of weaving strong validity arguments. It is also important to note that while Kirkhart's multicultural validity framework approaches validity through a cultural lens, it was still developed within a Western perspective and may therefore be an inadequate representation of validity from an indigenous perspective.

Guardianship and Issues of Sovereignty

The historical record of the use and effects of evaluation among Indian communities has often resulted in marginalizing tribal communities and peoples. For example, when being compared to standardized norms of educational performance, Indian children and youth are labeled as underperforming, as these norms do not consider the special gifts of individual students. The consequences of this historical record have resulted in skepticism among indigenous peoples about the value of evaluation. IEF was built around a reaffirmation of cultural values in the practice of evaluation in indigenous communities. Furthermore, the role of evaluator within those communities comes with great responsibility. Kovach (2010) notes that "[a] researcher assumes a responsibility that the story shared will be treated with the respect it deserves in acknowledgment of the relationship from which it emerges" (p. 97). The IEF is based on a core value of commitment to tribal sovereignty, especially regarding "ownership" of evaluation data and of the evaluation product itself. Indigenous evaluators must take special guard to ensure that the uses of their work are in concert with tribal values and respectful of the nation-building aspect of evaluation.

The implications and limitations of the IEF for evaluation practice within and outside of American Indian contexts are also worth consideration. It has been noted that the IEF utilizes a definition of knowledge that is considerably different from the Western research model. Knowledge, for example, may be derived from spiritual sources and involves the use of cultural protocols that may be specific to particular tribal settings. The IEF, therefore, may not always be applicable outside indigenous settings. Great care and consideration should be given to adaptation of the IEF practices and methods. As Kovach notes, "story, as a method, is used differently from culture to culture, and so its application falters without full appreciation of the underlying epistemological assumptions that motivate its use" (2010, pp. 96–97). Although the IEF may be adapted to other settings, it should be understood that there would be a fundamental adjustment in its epistemological grounding.

Reflections on Rog's Context of Evaluation Model

The IEF described here offers strong support for Rog's argument that considerations of both evaluation context and setting profoundly influence method choice and implementation. The importance of putting context ahead of method choice cannot be overstated. Rog (2009) expertly illustrates the limitations of a methods-first approach to effectiveness evaluation, showing how it can lead to avoiding important questions. She proposes an alternative to a methods-first approach, which she labels *context-sensitive evaluation practice*. IEF is certainly congruent with this conceptualization.

IEF also suggests another interpretation, one that takes the argument even further and suggests that, despite its strengths, Rog's model still significantly underestimates the impact of cultural context. Context goes beyond notions of accommodation and adaptation to contextual conditions; rather, it defines the entire evaluation landscape, including how it is viewed, understood, designed, performed, and used.

Rog (2009) places context alongside relevance and rigor in pursuit of actionable evidence, but indigenous evaluation tells a different story, one in which context plays an even larger role. Rather than sitting alongside relevance and rigor, context actually *defines* them. Moreover, context also defines what counts as actionable evidence, the ultimate end of Rog's model. Relevance, rigor, and actionable evidence are all culturally and contextually located, defined by values, assumptions, and circumstances. None can be understood outside of context. We propose that this holds true for all evaluation; however, context may often go unrecognized, unnamed, and unexamined, as Rog has noted. IEF makes it visible and its role explicit.

Rog has advanced considerations of context from background to foreground, from a character role to a leading role in our evaluations. An indigenous framing of evaluation illustrates how context in fact writes the script and staging and directs the entire performance.

References

Basso, K. H. (1996). *Wisdom sits in places: Landscape and language among the Western Apache*. Albuquerque, NM: University of New Mexico Press.

Cajete, G. (2000). *Native science: Natural laws of interdependence*. Santa Fe, NM: Clear Light Publishers.

Chen, H. T., Donaldson, S. I., & Mark, M. M. (2011). Validity frameworks for outcome evaluation. In H. T. Chen, S. I. Donaldson, & M. M. Mark (Eds.), *Advancing validity in outcome evaluation: Theory and practice. New Directions for Evaluation, 130*, 5–16.

Davis, C., Long Feather, C., & Padmanabhan, G. (2007). *North Dakota Tribal College Faculty Research Model; Guiding undergraduate student research in science, technology, engineering, and mathematics*. Retrieved from http://www.ndsu.edu/epscor/NATURE /Documents/NDTribalCollegeFacultyResearchModel_8-30-07_final.pdf

Deloria, V., Jr. (1999). If you think about it, you will see that it is true. In B. Deloria, K. Foehner, & S. Scinta (Eds.), *Spirit and reason: The Vine Deloria, Jr. Reader* (pp. 40–60). Golden, CO: Fulcrum Publishing.

Estrada, V. M. Jiménez. (2005). The Tree of Life as a research methodology. *The Australian Journal of Indigenous Education, 34*, 44–52.

Frank, D. T. (2010). *Integrating Lakota culture and biological science into a holistic research methodology: Lakol wico un na wico han wopasi* (Unpublished doctoral dissertation). South Dakota State University, Brookings.

Johnson, E. C., Kirkhart, K. E., Madison, A. M., Noley, G. B., & Solano-Flores, G. (2008). The impact of narrow views of scientific rigor on evaluation practices for underrepresented groups. In N. L. Smith & P. R. Brandon (Ed.), *Fundamental issues in evaluation* (pp. 197–218). New York, NY: Guilford Press.

Kirkhart, K. E. (1995). Seeking multicultural validity: A postcard from the road. *Evaluation Practice, 16*(1), 1–12.

Kirkhart, K. E. (2005). Through a cultural lens: Reflections on validity and theory in evaluation. In S. Hood, R. Hopson, & H. Frierson (Eds.), *The role of culture and cultural context: A mandate for inclusion, the discovery of truth, and understanding in evaluative theory and practice* (pp. 21–39). Greenwich, CT: Information Age Publishing.

Kirkhart, K. E. (2010). Eyes on the prize: Multicultural validity and evaluation theory. *American Journal of Evaluation, 31*(3), 400–413.

Kovach, M. (2010). *Indigenous methodologies: Characteristics, conversations, and contexts.* Toronto, Ontario, Canada: University of Toronto Press.

LaFrance, J., & Crazy Bull, C. (2009). Researching ourselves back to life: Taking control of the research agenda in Indian country. In D. M. Mertens & P. E. Ginsberg (Eds.), *The handbook of social research ethics* (pp. 135–149). Thousand Oaks, CA: SAGE.

LaFrance, J., & Nichols, R. (2009). *Indigenous evaluation framework: Telling our story in our place and time.* Alexandria, VA: American Indian Higher Education Consortium (AIHEC).

Robertson, P., Jorgenson, M., & Garrow, C. (2004). Indigenizing evaluation research: How Lakota methodologies are helping "raise the tipi" in the Oglala Sioux Nation. *The American Indian Quarterly, 28*(3–4), 499–526.

Rog, D. J. (2009, November). *Toward context-sensitive evaluation practice.* Presidential address. Evaluation 2009: 23rd annual conference of the American Evaluation Association, Orlando, FL.

Rog, D. J. (2011, November). *Balancing rigor, relevance and reason: Fitting methods to the context.* Paper presented as part of the panel, Valuing our Methodological Diversity (Jennifer C. Greene, Chair). Evaluation 2011: 25th Annual Conference of the American Evaluation Association, Anaheim, CA.

Rosaldo, R. (1993). *Culture and truth: The remaking of social analysis.* Boston, MA: Beacon Press.

Ross, R. (1992). *Dancing with a ghost: Explaining Indian reality.* Markham, Ontario, Canada: Octopus.

Weber-Pillwax, C. (1999). Indigenous research methodology: Exploratory discussion of an elusive subject. *Journal of Educational Thought, 33*(1), 31–45.

Wilson, S. (2008). *Research is ceremony: Indigenous research methods.* Halifax, Canada: Fernwood.

Endnote

The protocol for introducing indigenous scholars includes their full name, tribal affiliation, family lineage, and geographic location of significance. We have honored this protocol although shortened it here to author's full name and tribal affiliation.

JOAN LAFRANCE *(Turtle Mountain Chippewa) is president, Mekinak Consulting, Seattle, Washington.*

RICHARD NICHOLS *(Santa Clara Pueblo/Tewa) is president, Colyer-Nichols, Inc., Fairview, New Mexico.*

KAREN E. KIRKHART *is professor, School of Social Work, Syracuse University, Syracuse, New York.*

5

Political Culture as Context for Evaluation

Peter Dahler-Larsen, Thomas A. Schwandt

Abstract

One way to understand the context of evaluation is in terms of its interaction with political culture. That culture includes citizens' views of the role of government and of evaluation and the history of the polity. This chapter illustrates the relationship of political culture and evaluation by means of two accounts of Danish political culture. The chapter also draws on this analysis to stimulate our thinking on the very idea of how context can be studied. © Wiley Periodicals, Inc., and the American Evaluation Association.

Context comes from the Latin word *contextus,* meaning "to join together" or "to weave together." It is a term that is constantly used but not easily explained. It is a term that can take on many meanings and has a significant history of investigation associated with it in different disciplines (e.g., in philosophy, Sharfstein, 1989; in anthropology, Dilley, 1999; in linguistics, Duranti & Goodwin, 1992; in political analysis, Tilly & Goodwin, 2006). In the English language, we use many synonyms for context, including setting, locale, situation, circumstances, milieu, and background—all of which carry somewhat different connotations. Context is associated with the broader idea of contextualism—the view that actions, expressions, behaviors, and so on can be understood only with reference to a specific context. In evaluation, this idea underlies some of the thinking about culturally responsive evaluation. A fairly common idea is that context is that which surrounds an object of interest and helps by its relevance to

NEW DIRECTIONS FOR EVALUATION, no. 135, Fall 2012   © Wiley Periodicals, Inc., and the American Evaluation Association.   Published online in Wiley Online Library (wileyonlinelibrary.com) • DOI: 10.1002/ev.20028 explain it (Sharfstein, 1989). Thus it is that we speak of an event, interpretation, or activity (such as an evaluation) taking place in a cultural context, historical context, social context, political context, religious context, linguistic context, institutional context, and so on. Or we can reference the linguistic, social, sociocultural, and spatiotemporal aspects of an action (like developing, implementing, or evaluating a policy or program). An important concern for evaluators is how to define what is relevant in a specific evaluation situation and how the weaving together of relevant contextual elements helps inform evaluative judgments on that occasion.

In this chapter we discuss the nature and practice of evaluation in the context of a political culture. Our primary purpose is to show that the concept of context is far more elusive, more indeterminable, and less object-like than it is often made out to be in discussions of evaluation context. We begin with two portrayals of the way an evaluator meets the Danish political culture.

The Political Culture in Denmark as a Context for Evaluation (Version I)

There is a unique political culture in Denmark. On the basis of both objective indicators and more ethnographic or impressionistic accounts, Danish political culture is renowned for its unique combination of equality, political participation, trust, public spending, and even happiness. This is due to both historical factors and a set of reinforcing interactions between the components in this unique configuration. As we would like to show, Denmark's cultural values are in close interplay with its political institutions.

Denmark is one of the oldest kingdoms in the world, counting a continued line of kings and queens for more than 1,000 years. Comparatively speaking, its population is fairly homogeneous and enjoys a sense of shared culture, language, and ethnicity. Institutional mechanisms over the years have undergirded this sense of collective identity. For example, alphabetization took place early in Denmark through collaboration between priests and schoolteachers at the local level, preparing the ground for a low-conflict culture based on general trust in shared rules and in both spiritual and earthly authorities (Knudsen, 1995).

A modern Danish democratic institution was established without bloodshed in 1848. The war with Prussia in 1864, which Denmark barely survived, invigorated a broad popular awakening emphasizing common destiny, values, and nationalism. Stories, songs, national symbols, collaborative forms of organization, and an active civil society helped pave the way for a unique self-understanding in Denmark. The small size of the country compared to nearby powerful neighbors, such as Germany and Russia, only reinforced the special sense of collective identity in Denmark.

In international comparisons over the years, the population of Denmark regularly comes out as one of the happiest peoples of the world

(Veenhoven, 1984). As one of the best explanations of this phenomenon, researchers point to the low income inequality in Denmark. Denmark's Gini coefficient (an internationally acknowledged indicator for income inequality that varies between 1 and 0 with lower scores reflecting less income inequality) is only 0.2 for Denmark compared to, for example, 0.4 for the United States (Alberti, 2011b). In a recent Wikipedia ranking, Denmark appeared as the most equal of 124 countries, whereas the United States took 92nd place.

Economic equality is related to values connected to egalitarianism and to low power distance (meaning that people with power are seen not to be very distant from the common man). Hofstede's (1999) international cultural surveys have demonstrated Denmark's characteristic score on both of these factors.

To achieve the goal of social equality, the state plays a major redistributive role. According to statistics for the Organization for Economic Cooperation and Development (OECD, 2006), the Danish state collects 48% of gross domestic product (GDP) in tax revenues (the corresponding figure is 24% in the United States). As a consequence, the marginal tax rate goes up to 63% in Denmark (vs. 35% in the United States) (Alberti, 2011c). In return, Danish citizens have free schools, hospitals, universities, and a number of other services such as unemployment benefits. Largely speaking, the strong redistributive role of the government is consistent with Danish values and with the wishes of the majority of the population. The term *welfare state* carries positive connotations to the vast majority of Danes. The majority of the dominant political parties offer only variations of packages of tax and service combinations; none of them include a dismantling of the welfare state in their political agendas.

In the most recent election (September, 2011), 87% of the Danes voted. There was no need to register as a voter. Since priests started keeping church books many centuries ago, Danes have known who the Danes are; thus the public administration nowadays automatically sends a voting card to each citizen above 18 years of age, thus symbolizing the universalistic and participatory nature of Danish democracy.

The Danish party system comprises about 10 parties, and it takes only 2% of the electoral vote to be represented in the parliament (called the Folketing). The principle of parliamentarianism reigns, meaning that the government cannot rule without the majority of the Folketing. Because no party alone holds a majority of the seats, more or less stable coalitions are formed. There is a continuous debate, and although government coalitions are formed, there is often an attempt to create different majorities on different issues. This constant negotiation process signifies both the multiplicity of viewpoints and the necessity of compromise and consensus. The Folketing is responsible for taxes as well as spending. Despite the large public sector in Denmark, the political system has kept public debt under much better control than that in many other countries (Kenworthy, 2011). The strong elements of involvement and participation in Danish political culture continue in the regional and municipal governments that administer most of the central welfare activities (such as school, social services, unemployment services, and health care) and allow for local democratic participation.

A strong characteristic of the political culture in Denmark is the high level of trust among citizens, both in terms of trust in public authorities and in other people in general (89% in general compared to 49% in the United States; Alberti, 2011b).

Researchers point to the interconnectedness of all these factors. Equality leads to trust, which together lead to participation. Egalitarianism and participation support public interventions that secure social and economic benefits for all. The welfare state supports a peaceful lifestyle based on nonviolence, low crime, trust, and dialogue. The institutional machinery undergirding these connections is, in turn, based on universalism, transparency, participation, and dialogue, thus creating a "virtuous circle."

It is in this broader context that Denmark (along with its fellow Scandinavian countries Norway and Sweden) has cultivated strong traditions for user involvement in public services. For example, in schools, parents and pupils have a role to play in user boards, pupils' councils, and so on. Even if there is no fee for schools and doctors, users of these services are free to choose which school and which doctor they want within certain practical limits. Denmark (along with Sweden and Norway) has been a leading country in developing evaluation models that invite users to participate in the evaluation of public services (Krogstrup, 1997; Vedung & Dahlberg, 2001). Philosophically, the inputs of users have been seen as a source of institutional renewal and innovation as well as a source of strengthening the overall democratic bonds that hold society together.

What is suggested here is a broad universe of social meanings as a specific political cultural context for evaluation. Users are not just recipients of services but human beings with the full rights of citizens. Participation and dialogue should be part of evaluation on the micro scale to symbolize the values of participation and dialogue on the macro scale. Public activities are not just programs that can be terminated at will, but the best attempts of the existing collective regime to extend its services to people in need, and to people who often have an unofficial or even legally mandated official right to receive these benefits. And the welfare state is by and large a positive phenomenon.

Within this political universe, it makes sense that there is no Danish word for *achievement* or for *performance*. However, there is a special term for everything that is considered to be originating in the people, that is, *folkelig*. The roots of the very same term are found in the Folkeskole (the universal primary school) as well as in the name of the parliament, the Folketing.

Evaluation practices that are consistent with this portrait of Danish political culture would likely take the universalistic and communitarian values undergirding the Danish welfare state as a normative starting point. Evaluation practice would also likely be egalitarian and participatory in its means. However, the presented version of Danish political culture is not the only one possible.

The Political Culture in Denmark as a Context for Evaluation (Version II)

The narrative in the preceding section is a favorite among Danish researchers who wish to publish their texts about the special Danish case. It is also a favorite among visitors to Denmark who bring home to their country the message that collectivist values do exist and public services can be seen as positive.

Yet, the previous story is at worst romantic and at best a highly selective version of reality. In fact, the traditional image of Danish political culture has come under intense pressure from at least three uncomfortable sources. Each of them has consequences for evaluation.

The first source of unrest is the increasing problems with financing the welfare state. Taxes (as a proportion of GDP) have not substantially gone up since the mid-1980s. Still, services seem to be in ever-increasing demand. A changing demographic composition of the Danish population leads to more recipients and fewer taxpayers. Medical technology and medicine become more and more expensive. The need for effective services and benchmarking is increasing.

The second source of change is international organizations. These organizations create a statistical space in which comparative statistics are not only commonplace, but also pave the way for competitive international policy making. Denmark is constantly responding to international comparisons flowing out of, for example, the European Union and OECD. These international organizations are not only providing statistical material with policy-making potential (Ozga, Dahler-Larsen, Segerholm, & Simola, 2011), they are also offering consultancy and policy advice. In several ways, evaluation regimes of international organizations are more or less integrated in Danish policy making.

The third source of change is increasing demands from users and citizens. Although some describe the welfare state as based on altruism and affection for one's neighbor, it is also, in practice, a huge insurance machine that serves all citizens. Especially in terms of crisis, each citizen is painfully aware of his/her payments to this machine as well as to the benefits received from it. Patients, parents, students, unemployed people, pensioners, and all other groups who receive benefits or might potentially receive benefits are articulate about their needs. User groups more often than not form professionally run organizations that function as interest groups in the political arena. If comparative information is available, it may be used as political ammunition by groups who feel they are being underserved or by journalists who portray all variation in services as social injustice.

Danish governments have responded quite actively to these challenges. Through an intense reform program, the whole administrative structure has been reorganized, reducing the number of municipalities in order to make administration more professional and efficient. Reforms have also led to changes in all policy areas that are central to the welfare state. Orientation toward the market as a central defining force in a globalized world is now a common feature among the major political forces in Denmark. Three examples illustrate this reformist movement: education, health care, and unemployment.

In education, international comparisons such as the Programme for International Student Assessment (PISA) have played a key role in redefining school policy. Their first function was to question the traditional view that Danish schools were the best in the world (without comparison [sic!]). Next, international comparisons intensified the need for data production about schools and the role of municipalities as school owners, thus pushing the need for accountability all the way down the implementation chain.

After OECD in 2004 recommended an "evaluation culture" in Danish education, grades, test results, and quality reports began to be published. Although educational researchers raised a critical voice in the early years of PISA, there is now a broad political consensus that the Danish school is one of the most important assets in the nation's competition internationally. It is now in the economic sense, not the cultural sense, that schools are seen to hold the key to the country's future.

In health care, intense financial pressures have led to an interest in quality management. A national model for quality measurement is inspired by international accreditation agencies and trends in performance management. A complicated array of contracts and performance indicators regulate the financial structure of each hospital and each ward.

In the area of unemployment, Denmark has intensified its active policy. The term *flexicurity* has been coined to denote a combination of easy layoff, easy retraining, and decent unemployment benefits (although time on unemployment benefits has been reduced). Specially designed projects for unemployed people are seen as necessary to make sure that they are trained and that the relative incentives for them still point in the direction of employment. The relatively high wages in Denmark (about 50% higher in entry-level jobs compared to the United States) can only be defended through constant training, reskilling, and incentives. So, Denmark has taken the high road to high wages (Alberti, 2011a), which is possible only if the state plays a very active role in the labor market. The case management of each unemployed person is controlled by job centers, which are, in turn, monitored closely. Each job center and each municipality is held accountable for its relative effectiveness on a large number of dimensions.

To sum up, the Danish polity has responded quickly and dramatically to the challenges posed by increasing demands, by international organizations, and by financial and market pressures. A wave of reforms all fit into a broad process of modernization in the public sector in Denmark.

The dominant forms of evaluation in this political context are quantitative, comparative, and oriented toward results, efficiency, and performance. Indicators reign. Users of public services do not play a major role. In unemployment services, their views do not count. In health and education, users are largely seen as consumers of services. Consumers are invited to inspect available comparative quality information on schools and hospitals before making their choices, but there is no participatory element in the dominant forms of evaluation. In fact, no major innovation in participatory and dialogue-oriented evaluation has been made in Denmark since 1998. Forms of evaluation consistent with the present political culture are those that build on performance management, indicators, benchmarking, and accreditation.

Understanding the Problematic Notion of "Context"

Our presentation of the two versions of political context sketched above is meant to emphasize the importance for evaluation of getting the context right. Yet such a task is far more complicated than much of the current evaluation literature makes it out to be, especially in view of attempts to conduct a contextual analysis that yields an inventory of types of context and their respective dimensions to which one then matches a suitable evaluation approach. The scenarios presented above demonstrate that how evaluators grasp and make sense of a particular context is not independent of how that context itself structures that understanding for them. Interests, cultures, ethos, norms, history, institutions, and the like are not static variables but dynamic, discursive, continually produced, and reproduced narratives that shape evaluators' views of the landscape in which they find themselves. In addition, evaluation contributes to context construction. Notice how forms and regimes of evaluation appear as elements of political culture in the two accounts above. At the same time, if one wants to justify a particular form of evaluation, a particular description of the context is a logical precondition. Evaluation practices do not simply interact with context; rather, context and evaluation practices are co-constructed.

In discussing the meaning of context to political analysis, Tilly and Goodwin (2006) argue that three classes of contextual effects matter in efforts to develop systematic descriptions and explanations of political processes: contextual effects on the analyst's understanding of political processes, contextual effects on the extent and type of evidence available on political processes, and contextual effects on the very political processes themselves. We believe a similar argument can be made for the relationship of context to systematic efforts to develop evaluations of programs and policies.

First, how an evaluator understands the context in which a particular evaluand is to be evaluated derives in part from the evaluator's involvement (or lack of involvement) with that evaluand. In other words, different kinds of involvements shape the evaluator's understanding. We offer two examples of what this means: In his first visits to Denmark, Schwandt saw what we portray in the first scenario described above. It was in terms of this scenario that he understood his involvement as an outsider to Danish culture. It was only after many more visits and extensive conversations with Danish colleagues that he came to recognize the Denmark portrayed in the second scenario and, hence, his understanding changed. A second example comes from arguments for cultural competence in evaluation. They rest on the very idea that an evaluator's familiarity and involvement with context is, at least in part, determinative of what he or she is able to see and comprehend. To understand context as an evaluator is not to understand it objectively, but to relate to it, engage in it, and build an evaluation on (only) those aspects of the context that are found pressing, interesting, relevant, or worthwhile.

Second, the particular kind of involvement that an evaluator has with an evaluand gives the evaluator access to (or prohibits the evaluator from gaining access to) certain kinds of evidence that other evaluators with different kinds of involvement may not (or may) have. The obvious case here has to do with evaluations conducted close up (i.e., the evaluator has intimate familiarity with the evaluand and can study it closely) or at a distance (i.e., the evaluator is largely physically removed from the workings of the evaluand and studies it at a distance). It is also evident when one considers the institutional location of an evaluator—for example, whether the evaluator is a private contractor, works for either a for-profit or nonprofit research and evaluation firm (e.g., AIR, WestSTAT, Urban Institute), works for the government (e.g., Government Accountability Office [GAO]), a nongovernment organization (NGO) (e.g., World Bank), and so on. Moreover, different types and sources of data pave the way for different descriptions of context. An example is the selective use of international comparative data in the two versions of Danish political context(s) above.

Third, as is quite obvious to any evaluator, evaluation processes themselves are shaped by contexts. In other words, before a given evaluation process unfolds, the context of the evaluand provides a set of understandings and forms of evidence available to the evaluator. In other words, the very evaluand itself is already contextualized. This is precisely the point of our two scenarios. It is also apparent in cross-cultural comparative studies of evaluation practices. For example, Radin (2003) explains that although Australia, New Zealand, and the United States use the same vocabulary for performance management and share a similar agenda, what the practice of performance management actually means cannot be comprehended without specific attention to the political cultures of each country.

Given the dynamic, discursive, and linguistic (not simply material) nature of context, a natural response is to attempt to identify, inventory, and manage the many contextual elements or dimensions one is presented with. Given the proclivity (at least in an ideal world) for rational decision-making models, it seems reasonable, on first glance, to attempt to analyze context in a relatively detached and calculative manner and then decide on an optimal approach for conducting an evaluation given the results of the contextual assessment. However, we are skeptical of the wisdom of such attempts and question efforts to perform contextual analysis that rest on reasoning such as the following:

- Evaluators, clients, and stakeholders live in a world of an objectively determined (or determinable) context for a given evaluation that reflects facts of the matter that are understood as relevant inputs, settings, demands, constraints, conditions, circumstances, and so on that in important ways affect the evaluation process. These include the demographic characteristics of actors in the setting as well as the actors' own cultural context; the material and economic features relevant to designing a specific evaluative investigation in the circumstances; the institutional and organizational climate in which the object of evaluation is embedded; interpersonal dynamics, and so on—and all of these considerations have both diachronic (historical) and synchronic (current point in time) aspects.
- If the evaluator can construct an inventory of these contextual factors, he or she will be able to grasp, in a fairly comprehensive way, the significance of the context for the evaluation.
- The evaluator has the capacity to appraise these factors in a deliberate and instrumental fashion so as to understand the effects of each on the choices he or she makes in the process of conducting an evaluation.
- Hence, problem-solving procedures can be designed that match understanding of context with evaluation approaches, in a fashion similar to matching research questions to research methods, leading to the choice of an optimal design for the evaluation process under various contextual circumstances.

We are, of course, sympathetic to the idea that evaluators should respond as carefully as possible to the specificities of context and avoid using the same approach to evaluation and the same investigative methods everywhere in an insensitive way. We are also in favor of using concept mapping and network analysis tools that help identify different political actors in any given policy environment and their position, power, and authority as well as to develop an understanding of policy networks and policy influencers that may impact the conduct and use of an evaluation (e.g., Bennett & Jessani, 2008;

Nash, Hudson, & Luttrell, 2006). However, we find the assumptions and way of reasoning listed above problematic in the following specific ways.

First, evaluators (and evaluations) do not simply identify and respond to contextual factors, but by virtue of their actions are always constructing, relating to, engaging in, and taking part in some reconstruction of the context in which they operate. Thus, for example, evaluators in the federal government in the United States are not only working in but also constructing and reconstructing a political context shaped, in part, by the Office of Management and Budget that oversees government agency program evaluation activities to determine their net effects, their success or failure, and how agencies respond to these findings by making management improvements and developing new budget and policy proposals. Evaluators both deal with a context that is already interpreted (politically constructed) in some particular way and contribute to its continued political reconstruction (Dilley, 2002). In contemporary political worlds, evaluation is a powerful managerial, organizational, and professional instrument that has helped shape and continues to shape the contexts in which a given generation of evaluators find themselves operating. An analysis that does not take into account the interactive and mutually constitutive relation between contexts and evaluation would, at minimum, be politically naïve. Such an analysis might also be morally naïve to the extent that it ignored the ways in which evaluation practice and context coconstruct the interests, needs, and obligations of program stakeholders, beneficiaries, and so forth (in this regard, consider for example how the coconstruction of evidence-based public health policy and practice creates one reality, whereas the co-construction of culturally responsive public health practice creates another).

Second, although it is clear that not all evaluation approaches, models, or designs are equally appropriate in all contexts, this does not mean that evaluators can readily turn to some kind of matching scheme when they want to know how a particular evaluation approach should be fit to a particular set of contextual factors. Different evaluation theories or approaches suggest, descriptively, how a configuration of politically relevant stakeholders and their considerations influence decision making, and normatively, how that should influence the involvement of those stakeholders in the evaluation process. Thus, evaluation theories and approaches (e.g., utilization focused, responsive, participatory, experimental, econometric, deliberative democratic, quality assurance) are already interpretations of the context, anchored in assumptions, generalizations, and experiences that particular evaluators have made and use in applying evaluation processes.

Third, the idea that evaluators can somehow simply observe the context of evaluation as if they were significantly detached from it is highly questionable. Although it is certainly the case that, in some situations, evaluators are brought into social and cultural circumstances that are foreign to them, it is also true that evaluators operate in organizational, managerial, and political contexts where they take for granted the majority of the assumptions made in the context in which they operate. This is especially true for evaluators working in political and administrative regimes where evaluation and performance measurement are already institutionalized to some degree and supported by organizational process and artifacts (indicators, handbooks, reporting and inspection systems, etc.). In these situations, the evaluator as an independent, rational, autonomous, and detached individual is an unrealistic abstraction. Rather, the evaluator already finds himself or herself embedded in and partially constituting the context.

Fourth, even if an evaluator could inventory contextual factors or dimensions, there is no guarantee that such a process would result in unequivocal and clear ways of making decisions about the evaluation. Three outcomes of contextual analysis are possible:

1. A contextual analysis may, in textbook fashion, lead to the recommendation of one and only one best way to evaluate under the circumstances without any tensions between the factors.
2. The choice of evaluation approach may be underdetermined by the contextual analysis, meaning that the evaluator is still left with some leeway in defining what he or she thinks is the best approach under the circumstances.
3. The choice of an evaluation approach may be overdetermined by the contextual analysis, meaning that no evaluation approach will sufficiently satisfy the many demands for various forms and uses of evaluation represented by the factors in the contextual analysis.

We believe the latter occurs so frequently that it can be regarded as normal. To evaluate is always to make some choices about which contextual factors to attend to and which to ignore.

Final Word

We have endeavored to show how context in and for evaluation, particularly with respect to the idea of political culture as context, is more complex, indeterminable, and far less easily managed and accounted for than we often take it to be. One could readily conclude from the foregoing that contingency theory—which holds that there is no one best way to evaluate—is what is required in view of our portrayal. In other words, one must fit the characteristics of the evaluation practice in question to the contingencies that reflect the situation (i.e., context) one is in. For such a theory to work, one needs to identify patterns of good fit between the situations (i.e., contexts) and the appropriate evaluation procedures. On the face of things, this is eminently sensible. However, what often happens is that situations or contexts are treated as given or fixed, thereby ignoring that the context or situation in question is complex, dynamic, and interpretable and that there may be contradictions within a particular context that make no choice of a particular response evident or obvious. The lesson here is something like this—although it seems quite reasonable to argue that evaluation is context dependent, we must be careful not to claim that we can neatly categorize contexts and then readily determine which evaluation approach offers the best fit. In our view, the responsibility of the evaluator does not start once the context has been precisely and correctly described. Instead, we view the interpretation and co-construction of contexts as an ever present and contestable element in the very practice of evaluation.

References

Alberti, M. (2011a, September). *The high road to high wages: Denmark's answer to the U.S. model*. Remapping Debate, New York. Retrieved from http://www.remapping debate.org/article/high-road-high-wages-denmarks-answerus-model

Alberti, M. (2011b, September). *Being a citizen, Danish style*. Remapping Debate, New York. Retrieved from http://www.remappingdebate.org/article/being-citizendanish-style

Alberti, M. (2011c, October). *Consider adapting Danish policy choices for U.S.? Centrists and conservatives say 'yes.'* Remapping Debate, New York. Retrieved from http://www .remappingdebate.org/article/consider-adapting-danish-policychoices-us-centrists-and-conservatives-say-yes/

Bennett, G., & Jessani, N. (Eds.). (2008). *The research matters knowledge translation toolkit*. International Development Research Center & the Swiss Agency for Development and Cooperation. Retrieved from http://www.who.int/pmnch/topics/2008_idrc _sdc/en/index.html

Dilley, R. M. (Ed.). (1999). *The problem of context*. New York, NY: Berghahn Books.

Dilley, R. M. (2002). The problem of context in social and cultural anthropology. *Language and Communication, 22*, 437–456.

Duranti, A., & Goodwin, C. (Eds.). (1992). *Rethinking context: Language as an interactive phenomenon*. Cambridge, United Kingdom: Cambridge University Press.

Hofstede, G. (1999). *Kulturer og organisationer. Overlevelse i en grænseoverskridende verden*. København, Denmark: Handelshøjskolens Forlag. [Cultures and Organizations]

Kenworthy, L. (2011, October). *Consider the evidence*. Retrieved from http://laneken worthy.net/category/economic-growth/

Knudsen, T. (1995). *Dansk statsbygning* [Building the Danish State]. København, Denmark: Jurist-og Økonomforbundets Forlag.

Krogstrup, H. K. (1997). User participation in quality assessment—A dialogue and learning oriented evaluation method. *Evaluation—The International Journal for Theory, Research and Practice, 3*(2), 205–224.

Nash, R., Hudson, A., & Luttrell, C. (2006). *Mapping political context: A toolkit for civil society organizations*. London, United Kingdom: Overseas Development Institute.

OECD. (2006). *OECD, Economic surveys Denmark*. OECD Publishing. Volume 2006/7—May 2006.

Ozga, J., Dahler-Larsen, P., Segerholm, C., & Simola, H. (2011). *Fabricating quality in education: Data and governance in Europe*. London, United Kingdom: Routledge.

Radin, B. A. (2003). A comparative approach to performance management: Contrasting the experience of Australia, New Zealand, and the United States. *International Journal of Public Administration, 26*(12), 1355–1376.

Sharfstein, B-A. (1989). *The dilemma of context.* New York, NY: New York University Press.

Tilly, C., & Goodwin, R. E. (Eds.). (2006). *Handbook of contextual political analysis.* Oxford, United Kingdom: Oxford University Press.

Vedung, E., & Dahlberg, M. (2001). *Demokrati och brukarutvärdering* [Democracy and user evaluation]. Lund, Sweden: Studentlitteratur.

Veenhoven, R. (1984). *Conditions of happiness.* Boston, MA: Reidel.

PETER DAHLER-LARSEN is a professor in the Department of Political Science and Public Management at the University of Southern Denmark.

THOMAS A. SCHWANDT is a professor in the Department of Educational Psychology and Senior Fellow at the Center for Culturally Responsive Evaluation and Assessment, University of Illinois at Urbana-Champaign.

Conner, R. F., Fitzpatrick, J. L., & Rog, D. J. (2012). A first step forward: Context assessment. In D. J. Rog, J. L. Fitzpatrick, & R. F. Conner (Eds.), *Context: A framework for its
influence on evaluation practice. New Directions for Evaluation, 135*, 89–105.

6

A First Step Forward:
Context Assessment

Ross F. Conner, Jody L. Fitzpatrick, Debra J. Rog

Abstract

*In this chapter, we revisit and expand the context framework of Debra Rog,
informed by three cases and by new aspects that we have identified. We then propose a way to move the framework into action, making context explicit. Based
on the framework's components, we describe and illustrate a process we label context assessment (CA), which provides a means of identifying important context-
related factors and integrating the implications of these within the three main
stages of evaluation.* © Wiley Periodicals, Inc., and the American Evaluation
Association.

The goal of this framework is to bring the topic of context into the
spotlight of evaluation concerns. Instead of treating context as an
occasional, optional secondary consideration in evaluation planning,
implementation, and utilization, we advocate placing context among the
primary considerations that are involved in the evaluation process. In this
concluding chapter we revisit the context framework, informed by the three
cases that have been presented and the new aspects that have been raised,
and describe the context assessment (CA) process, which provides a means
of integrating context within the important stages of evaluation.

Revisiting the Context Framework

In her context framework, originally presented as the presidential address at the 2009 American Evaluation Association (Rog, 2009) and elaborated in this issue (Rog, 2012), Rog describes five areas to attend to: the nature of the particular phenomenon or problem, the nature of the intervention, the broader environment in which the intervention is set, the parameters of the evaluation itself, and the broader decision-making arena. Within each of these areas, she specifies seven dimensions to examine: physical, organizational, social, cultural, traditional, political, and historical. In addition, within some of these dimensions, particularly the social and cultural, Rog notes that there are additional subdimensions that may be applicable: demographic issues of gender, race, and language, as well as issues of power differences, class, other denominators of equity, and sociopolitical status. The possible dimensions and subdimensions focus on different aspects, ranging from those that are program client related, to those that are program related, and to those that are much broader, such as the environment surrounding the program, including both physical characteristics and general cultural and political aspects. Not all dimensions and subdimensions are equally relevant in any particular program and its evaluation; it depends on the context, as the examples below demonstrate.

Applying the Framework in Three Cases

The examples provided in Chapters 3–5 illustrate how different areas and dimensions emerge as important to evaluation practice in three different settings. The example from Thurston, Smith, Genskow, Prokopy, and Hargrove (2012) focuses on the environmental area and the phenomenon of water quality. Although the authors describe how each area of Rog's framework impacts their evaluation of watersheds, the most important contextual influences are the nature of the problem or phenomenon and the interventions themselves. These writers describe well the complex nature of the phenomenon/problem and how it impacts evaluation choices. Environmental decision makers have defined the problem as water quality within a watershed. A watershed is a large geographical area identified by the water that comes in (rain and snow) and goes out of an area (streams ending in a body of water). Consequently, a watershed often crosses established jurisdictional lines that complicate the formation of policies and programs and the evaluation itself. Further, watersheds may be nested within each other. One evaluation may focus on the smallest part of the watershed, water entering a relatively small body of water and its sources; another might focus on the larger watershed, water entering a large lake or ocean and all its sources. It is important for the evaluator to consider the physical, organizational, cultural, political, and historic implications of the boundaries in order to consider who should be involved as stakeholders in the evaluation, who might be sources of data, who might have an interest in the results, who might object to the evaluation, and so forth.

The context of the intervention also has effects on the evaluation. Thurston and her coauthors highlight the challenges in evaluating interventions that may take years to have an effect, during which time the contextual factors will likely shift in ways that can affect the evaluation. Evaluators may, therefore, turn to shorter-term, intermediate measures of outcomes, framed as the earlier steps in the logic model. In the area of water quality, this means moving toward using social indicators as a measure of change in addition to the more long-term, ultimately desired physical changes in the water quality. Here, Thurston and her colleagues encounter another inevitable contextual factor, decision makers' and stakeholders' values and beliefs concerning appropriate measures. In water quality, the measures traditionally have been of chemical elements that indicate water quality. Because of their education, training, and culture, many of the typical water quality area stakeholders question and resist measures that are not seen as traditionally scientific, so social indicators present a problem for these stakeholders. Evaluators must work to understand these cultural views and to educate and persuade users and decision makers of the validity and necessity of these measures for assessing more proximal outcomes.

The chapter by LaFrance, Nichols, and Kirkhart (2012) also illustrates how Rog's five areas are relevant to an evaluation process. These evaluators provide a particularly good example of the ways in which two of the five framework areas interact: the broader environment in which the intervention is set and the parameters of the evaluation itself. In addition, they put primary importance on the cultural dimensions within these two areas. In the American Indian environment that is the primary setting for their examples, the cultural factors are so central that these issues write the script, as they say, for many aspects of the evaluation, including even such basic aspects as the epistemology that applies. For example, they explain how American Indian ways of knowing and understanding are circular and contributive, not linear and causative, as are postpositivist evaluation approaches that play a prominent role in evaluation. LaFrance and her colleagues describe other aspects of the American Indian culture that relate to the implementation of evaluation, such as the importance of stories and the utility of cultural metaphors as ways of learning and understanding.

In evaluations of American Indian communities, LaFrance and her colleagues see the contextual element of the culture of the participants and community as critical factors for the evaluator to consider. This illustrates how other evaluators, working on evaluation projects that have American Indian communities as one of the primary stakeholder groups, can benefit from careful attention to the broader environment and factors within it. The challenge for many evaluation projects is that several important stakeholder groups are frequently involved, and these stakeholder groups often have different and sometimes conflicting views of the contextual factors. For example,

Thurston and her colleagues working in water quality contexts may have American Indian groups as one important stakeholder group involved in an evaluation project of a large watershed, but they also have others, such as business groups or laboratory scientists. These different stakeholder groups have different backgrounds and different understandings about important contextual issues, such as what constitutes credible evidence. An evaluator taking a context-sensitive approach to evaluation planning, implementation, and results utilization will be on the lookout for and explore these different realities, assumptions, and priorities in the primary stakeholder groups. With a good understanding of the important similarities and differences, the evaluator can build on the similarities and then work with the primary stakeholder groups to help them understand the differences and also understand the compromises made among them, in order to craft an evaluation plan that will best suit the context. This is not to say that this is an easy process; it takes time, attention, and careful consideration but it has the benefit of transparently weighing and resolving conflicting perspectives at the outset, increasing the chances that the evaluation will be implemented successfully and validly and then be used by the primary stakeholders.

The importance of the fifth area of Rog's framework, the broader decision-making arena and its historic and cultural context, is well illustrated by Dahler-Larsen and Schwandt (2012). Their chapter demonstrates how citizens' views of the roles of government and expectations of evaluation influence the actual practice of evaluation. They describe two versions of the Danish political culture. Historically, Denmark has been a relatively homogeneous country with trust among citizens and trust in the government. Citizens saw the government's role as helping those in need and avoiding serious income inequality. Under this first view of Danish political culture, evaluations were not done to cut programs and accountability was not a concern. Evaluations, instead, were to obtain citizen and user input, in a very participatory culture, to improve programs. More recently, a second view of political culture has emerged, which is probably now blending with the first. The culture has changed for several reasons that commonly affect political culture. Financing of the welfare state became more difficult amid increasing demands from users. Further, international organizations such as the European Union and the Organization for Economic Cooperation and Development began to make cross-country statistical comparisons that made Danes more concerned with their status among other countries. In particular, Danish citizens and government officials became concerned with the quality of their schools and of their health care. These changes prompted a new direction in evaluation, one more focused on outcomes and quality measurement and less concerned with participatory elements of evaluation. These changes illustrate the strong influence of political culture, and changes in that culture, on the focus and conduct of evaluation.

New Directions for Evaluation • DOI: 10.1002/ev

Dahler-Larson and Schwandt also discuss the broader elements of context in evaluation. They recognize the importance of understanding context but question whether it can be known and how it can be known. They note that context is complicated and dynamic, changing in response to time and many other variables, and, in fact, their two scenarios of the Danish political culture reveal that complexity and dynamism. We agree, but we believe the complexity and dynamism do not negate the need for the evaluator to attempt to identify elements of context that may influence their evaluation.

Using Context Assessment

Context is indeed complex, multidimensional, dynamic, and difficult to get right. It likely is not even possible to get the context completely right, but this is not a limitation. Even if possible, it would not be desirable to delineate an objective, complete inventory of all contextual elements relevant to an evaluation because of the time and resources this would require. Our aim in advocating CA is to prompt evaluators to consider context more explicitly and carefully than they have in the past, beyond a set of variables that need to controlled and isolated. CA will not be entirely objective nor will it be independent: Context will influence the evaluators' views and the evaluation will influence the context.

CA, as described in more detail below, is intended to prompt evaluators to consider which elements of context might be most important for the evaluator to consider at different stages of a particular evaluation, from planning to implementation to results utilization and decision making. The three cases illustrate the advantages of considering important areas of context. In evaluations of American Indian communities, LaFrance and her colleagues see the contextual elements of the culture of the participants and community as critical elements for the evaluator to consider. These contextual elements also may be important to watershed evaluations like those of Thurston and her colleagues, but they are less so than the cultural and traditional elements of the broader environment that concern differing views of water, land, and credible data. Overlapping jurisdictions and defining the problem area are important contextual elements for Thurston and her fellow evaluators. Working with a different set of important contextual elements, Dahler-Larsen and Schwandt highlight the importance of the new political culture in Denmark in understanding the current emphases of social program evaluations, particularly school evaluations. As these three cases illustrate, evaluators do not need to catalogue all elements of context, but instead focus on those they identify as most relevant; it is these they will concentrate on because these could most affect the program, the stakeholders, and the evaluation.

How do evaluators learn about these important contextual factors? We have reports from evaluators that shed light on this question, as they describe the processes that they go through in conducting evaluation. Interviews of evaluators by Fitzpatrick, Christie, and Mark (2009) illustrate how some evaluators become context sensitive. In addition to learning more about the intervention, these evaluators initially become very familiar with the context areas of the phenomenon/problem and the broader environment surrounding the intervention, in all its dimensions. Good examples of this are Bledsoe learning about the Newark neighborhood of the program she evaluated, and Riccio and his team learning about different counties in California in their implementation of welfare reform (Fitzpatrick et al., 2009). After they are very familiar with many contextual factors, skilled context-sensitive evaluators are then able to identify a few particularly important contextual elements related to their evaluation. They do not select an evaluation model based on these insights, but, rather, they shape the focus of their evaluation, their means of data collection, analysis and interpretation, and their methods of dissemination based on their understanding of the critical elements of the context.

Extending the Framework

The examples and issues raised by these three cases illustrate and provide good ideas about extending the basic five-area formulation; in addition, they include some cautions about applying a context-sensitive framework to an evaluation project. The five areas remain the same: the general phenomenon or issue, the particular intervention, the broad environment in which the intervention is set, the parameters of the evaluation itself, and the broad decision-making arena. In three of these, the focus is broader (phenomenon, intervention environment, and decision-making arena); in two, the focus is narrower (intervention and evaluation), although importantly informed by the broader assessment in the other three areas. Within each area, Rog highlighted dimensions and subdimensions that might be relevant, some focused on groups or organizations (e.g., political) and others focused on individuals (e.g., gender). In addition, the evaluator needs to be attuned to other possible aspects of context (e.g., ideas about what constitutes valid information) that are relevant to evaluation. Aspects such as these are hard to categorize a priori and can take on a different character, depending on the situation, but, if one is sensitive to and explicitly watching for important contextual factors, they become apparent. It is necessary to understand these special social realities and social constructs if an evaluation is to go forward.

These dimensions and subdimensions, both those that we can categorize and those that are less tangible, do not apply to each of the five areas; physical aspects, for example, are not applicable to the evaluation area or to the decision-making area. These dimensions and subdimensions are not proposed as necessary aspects in all areas but instead as suggestive aspects, to

NEW DIRECTIONS FOR EVALUATION • DOI: 10.1002/ev

be considered if relevant to a particular context. We also recognize that settings are dynamic and therefore that at least some relevant contextual aspects are likely to change over time. This means that CA cannot be a one-time process, although the initial assessment would be the most important and most intensive. Briefer CA checks can be made at several points in the typical evaluation process, either to add new evaluation components that address new important dimensions or to deemphasize or even drop evaluation components that no longer are relevant.

We do not advocate that the framework be used in a rigid manner. Instead, we believe it provides a conceptual framework that will increase evaluators' awareness of context's consequences in the evaluation process, and it also provides a simple schema that evaluators can apply to move this awareness into action, through context assessment. In the next section, we describe how the framework can be applied.

Applying Context Assessment in Evaluation

Our intent in focusing on context in evaluation is to raise the profile of this issue in the general evaluation process. Although often mentioned in passing in many evaluations and occasionally attended to more seriously in a few evaluations, context has not received the prominence that we believe it should have among the set of primary evaluation issues that guide evaluation planning, implementation, and utilization/decision making. To change this, we propose a three-step process for context assessment (CA) that could make it a part of the standard procedures that are typically involved in the three main evaluation steps: planning, implementation, and use/decision making. Below, we describe the application of CA to each step, illustrating each one through an example. At the end, we discuss the benefits, limitations, and challenges of doing CA.

The example used in each step is hypothetical but based on actual experiences we have had conducting evaluations, combined to make the example more representative. Nonetheless, we realize that no one example can encompass most evaluation situations. Rather than focus on the limitations of the example, we encourage readers to use the example as a way to understand better what we intend for the content of a context assessment.

Step 1: Context Assessment for Evaluation Planning

During the first step of the typical evaluation process, there is a planning phase to identify and understand the evaluation questions and issues. In a simple case, the people who are planning for or already operating the program meet with the evaluators to share information about the program and their view of the key evaluation questions and issues. An explicit CA could be conducted during and around these planning meetings, with the use of the sample questions in Table 6.1.

Table 6.1. Context Assessment During Evaluation Planning

Area	Sample Guiding Questions
General phenomenon/problem	What is the problem the program is addressing? How did it emerge? How long has it existed? What groups prompted concern about it? What is already known about it? What are the dominant methods used for understanding the phenomenon/problem? What tools exist for measuring change?
Particular intervention	Where is the program in its life cycle? How is the program structured? What are the different components and how do they fit in the broader environment? Who does the program serve? What are their characteristics, beliefs, culture, needs, and desired outcomes?
Broad environment around the intervention	What are the different layers of environment that affect and can be affected by the intervention? What aspects of these different climates are affecting the design and operation of the program? What are important historical, social, and cultural elements of the community in which the program is conducted? Are there political or social views that affect perspectives on the program, its clients, or decision makers?
Parameters of the evaluation	What are the primary and secondary evaluation questions and their implications for possible methodology and design choices? What resources are available to support the evaluation (e.g., budget, time frame, local evaluation capacity, evaluation ethos)?
Broad decision-making arena	Who are the main decision makers/users of the evaluation information? What are their views, values, and history about the program, and about evaluation? What is the larger political culture in which they work? What are the expectations of their organization? What are the expectations of citizens they serve regarding government programs, and about evaluation? What are the political expectations for evaluation?

Let us illustrate these questions by introducing our example, which focuses on a health issue. Through the answers to these questions, you will begin to understand the example and its different aspects, much as you would when applying context assessment to an actual case. The first area of questioning focuses on the general phenomenon or problem and the main issues related to it. In our example, the problem is cancer among women. Regarding this general problem, the main issues are the high prevalence of breast and cervical cancer (among other types of cancers), the existence of screening programs for breast and cervical cancers in women, and the existence of treatment programs for these cancers. Other important aspects related to this issue are the public's general high level of awareness of cancer as a health problem, particularly breast cancer among women, thanks to the Pink Ribbon campaign; and the persistence of some misconceptions about cancer, its causes, consequences, and treatments, particularly among some subpopulations.

The second area of CA questioning focuses on the particular intervention. In this example, the program is focused on breast and cervical cancer control in women in a Chinese American community. The program developers were aware not only of the high prevalence of breast and cervical cancer among women, but also of the higher-than-average death rates among those affected in the Chinese American community. The reasons for this relate to limited or very late-stage cancer screening due to a general stigma associated with disease of any type, particularly with deadly diseases, and this stigma not only is attached to the individual herself but also to her family, both immediate and extended. The social pressure in the community, therefore, is not to recognize disease of any type but instead to ignore it and, if identified, to hide it. An additional factor in the local community is that most local Chinese American doctors are men, so a breast-screening procedure conducted by men (even medically trained) on women is socially and personally awkward, at best. Developed with significant community input as well as university-based health promotion experts, the intervention program focused on reducing the stigma of cancer and increasing the presence of female screeners (doctors and nurses) as a way to increase regular and early screenings so that cancers could be identified early, when treatment can be successful and save lives. The program focused on recruiting respected members of the Chinese American community to speak publicly about cancer, including their own personal experiences with it, and on training doctors and nurses, particularly women, about screening procedures for Chinese American women in the local community, then using them in special screening events.

The third area of CA involves the broad environment around the intervention. In this example, important factors were the existence of a well-respected, well-established, and well-connected Asian American community-based organization working on health issues (broadly defined) in this community (as well as in other Asian communities in the area), and the existence of a health-care system in the area with outreach to and experience with the Chinese American community. Another important issue was the existence of several foundations and government agencies that had resources to support cancer control efforts in diverse communities, as well as the presence of several colleges and universities with students and professors attuned to and connected with community health and the Asian subpopulations.

New Directions for Evaluation • DOI: 10.1002/ev

The fourth area of CA questioning relates to the parameters of the evaluation. At the outset, there was a diverse group of interested stakeholders, very importantly including Chinese American women from the community, but also funders, and government agency staff; in addition, other interested stakeholders were men and women in the Asian community locally, nationally, and even internationally. Among these stakeholders there was general agreement that evaluation questions and answers should focus on changes in the number and characteristics of the women who received screenings (these data were surrogate measures of changes in perceptions of stigma) and on the outcomes of those screenings, not only in terms of cancers identified but also in terms of cancers ended. These stakeholders generally agreed on the need for both quantitative and qualitative data, both formative and summative. Even more than the funders and agency personnel, the women from the community were very strong advocates for impact-oriented data and for evaluation designs that would provide it (the reason: they wanted to be sure that they were improving the situation for women in the community, which was the main goal of the program and the evaluation). For baseline comparative information, the evaluation benefited from random surveys about cancers among minority communities that were collected each year through a state health agency.

Finally, the fifth area of CA inquiry focuses on the broad decision-making arena and those who will use the evaluation findings. In the cancer control intervention, the same groups of stakeholders mentioned for the fourth area were relevant here. Three groups were particularly relevant and could be considered the main users: women leaders in the Chinese American community in the area, the funders, and those within the university/college group with special interest in community health and/or disparities in Asian health care. However, there were other stakeholders attending to the intervention and its results, including some in China and other places throughout the United States. These other, distant stakeholders were connected electronically to the program staff and some participants. Because of this, some program materials (e.g., cancer materials in Chinese) were made available to others via the Internet.

To summarize, the aim of context assessment at the first stage of the evaluation process is to sensitize the evaluator to aspects of the context, at various levels and in different areas, that need to be considered as evaluation planning proceeds. As the above example of the Chinese American women's cancer control intervention demonstrates, many of the issues are similar to those an evaluator without a particular context focus might encounter. What is important for a context assessment is what is done next. The evaluator focuses specifically on answering this question: What are the implications for evaluation planning, implementation, and use based on the most important context issues identified across the five areas? In the cancer control example, these were some of those implications for evaluation planning. Regarding perspectives and participants, Chinese American women should be centrally involved in all steps in the process, as critical stakeholders; in addition, funders, agency personnel, and college/university members are important stakeholders and contributors. Regarding methods, the main focuses needed to be on outputs (i.e., numbers of screenings) and outcomes (i.e., cancer identification and treatment as needed), as well as on impacts to the extent possible, within the evaluation budget. Regarding important decision makers and users, women leaders in the Chinese American community, both at the local and state levels, were closely watching for results, as were the funders, health agency personnel, and university/college health researchers. The program intervention staff and volunteers were other important users; they were strong evaluation supporters, ready to use formative information to adjust the program components and to use summative information to confirm outcomes and impacts.

Step 2: Context Assessment for Evaluation Implementation

During the second step of the typical general evaluation process, the evaluation begins to be implemented. Context assessment changes during this step to a periodic monitoring of the five areas, where the aim is to identify any important changes in contextual elements that could have an effect on the evaluation. The general question guiding CA is this: Have new contextual elements arisen that affect the decisions made during the earlier planning step, particularly about the implications for the conduct and use of the evaluation? If so, what changes are needed? Table 6.2 lists general questions that would be considered at this step for each of the five areas.

Depending on the complexity and scale of the intervention and on the context in which it is set, the answers to many of these guiding questions may or may not require any changes. As noted above, CA conducted during this second step is more like monitoring, to be sure that salient issues are still the same and that decisions for the evaluation made based on them are still the best ones. This analysis can be done quickly but it also should be done explicitly, giving the evaluator (and possibly other important stakeholders who could be included in the CA discussions) an opportunity to pull back from the day-to-day demands and obligations of the evaluation and to again take the broad, overarching view, with the contextual elements providing the anchors.

Let us illustrate how this second part of the contextual assessment can proceed using the example of the Chinese American cancer control intervention. Consider these two contextual elements that might hypothetically occur: A new particularly effective cancer curative drug is released, and a cancer-survivor woman in the local Chinese American community becomes a very public face of the intervention message and benefits. These elements relate to the first framework area (general phenomenon/problem), to the second

Table 6.2. Context Assessment During Evaluation Implementation

Area	Sample Guiding Questions
General phenomenon/problem	Have new aspects related to the phenomenon/problem been identified or arisen? Have we learned more about the phenomenon or the problem that may influence our approach? Has new knowledge been gathered through other research and evaluation that may have a bearing on this evaluation or on stakeholders' receptivity to findings?
Particular intervention	Have new intervention components been added/modified/eliminated that affect the intervention? Has the level of intensity of the intervention changed because of funding increases or decreases?
Broad environment around the intervention	Have new relevant events, people, or issues arisen in the general environment in which the intervention is anchored? Do these new factors have implications for the intervention and/or its evaluation?
Parameters of the evaluation	Do the main evaluation components continue to be responsive to the relevant contextual factors? Have the budget, time, and so on changed in any way?
Broad decision-making arena	Have new organizations or individuals, with different perspectives, entered the decision-making arena, and do these new factors need to be addressed? Have the needs of decision makers changed in any way that might impact the evaluation or receptivity to the findings?

area (particular intervention), to the third (broader environment), with implications for the fourth (parameters of the evaluation). This drug release would likely change the Chinese American community's assessment of the degree of stigma associated with cancer, likely lowering the stigma because death would be less certain. The drug would also bolster the intervention program's advocacy of screening procedures, given the new effective treatment that is now available. The effects of knowledge of this new drug on women's choices to be screened might result in more screenings (if some women think they should be screened sooner) or possibly in reduced screenings (if some women now think they can delay screening without health consequences). The appearance of a new public Chinese American face for the intervention message could have a direct effect on the intervention program's target population, resulting in increased awareness of the issues, increased belief in cancer's curability if detected, and decreased concerns about long-term stigma; all of these changes could lead to more women in the community being screened and doing this earlier rather than later. The implications for the evaluation are that an increase in program screenings, possibly a dramatic increase, could be detected in the monthly cancer screening data that the program is routinely collecting as part of the evaluation. This is an example not only of the necessity but also of the benefit of being aware of changing contextual factors. A sudden increase in screenings, occurring at the same time as one or both of these two new context factors begin to operate, provides an unexpected opportunity to evaluate the effects of this mini intervention within the regular intervention, bolstering the program's theory of change.

By recognizing changes like these in the context, the evaluator is in a better position to adjust measurements to pick up the changes and to capitalize on new design opportunities to detect program-related changes better. If conscious note is taken and new evaluation components added when contextual changes such as these occur, the evaluator can, for example, add new comparison conditions within the design that allow a before–after assessment of the effects of the new contextual elements. On its own, such a before–after measure has limitations but, in combination with other design components and measurements, it can add evidence to explain what parts of the intervention are more and less successful.

Step 3: Context Assessment for Evaluation Decision Making and Use

During the final step of the typical general evaluation process, the evaluation findings are considered by decision makers and possibly put into use, both instrumental and conceptual. At this point in the process, CA becomes more limited, focused primarily on two of the five main areas: the broad environment around the intervention and the decision-making arena, although aspects of the phenomenon/problem might also be considered for certain actions, such as making recommendations. At this late step in the generic evaluation process, the contextual implications of two of the areas (intervention and evaluation) are no longer relevant; they were incorporated into the two earlier steps.

As shown in Table 6.3, two main areas are the focus during this third step: the broad environment around the intervention and the broad decision-making arena. In both areas there are questions about adjustments that are needed in the decisions made in the two earlier steps of the contextual assessment about which stakeholders from both of these areas were primary and needed to be involved. Particularly for long interventions and for large, geographically spread interventions, the most relevant stakeholders in these two areas may change, possibly resulting in new perspectives and values that need to be considered and included in making recommendations or discussing next steps.

Table 6.3. Context Assessment During Evaluation Decision Making and Use

Area	Sample Guiding Questions
Broad environment around the intervention	Are the original stakeholders still relevant? What new stakeholders need to be added? Related to the content of recommendations that might be made, is the infrastructure in place and are resources (staff, materials, support) available to provide the actions and services that will be recommended? Might these resources be drawn away from other, unrelated programs, possibly jeopardizing them?
Broad decision-making arena	How has the arena changed since the outset of evaluation planning? Should other important stakeholders be included? How are decision makers responding to the evaluation? How are they using it? What elements receive the most attention from various stakeholders and decision makers? How do their values, position, or history affect their use of the information? Are there other dissemination or communication strategies that might increase their use?

It is important to note that there is a second category of questions that probably were not considered closely in the two earlier steps of CA; these CA questions relate to follow-on issues that will become important if evaluation recommendations are carried out. For example, referencing the Chinese American cancer-screening program one last time, if the program evaluation results demonstrate that the program is a success, are there new resources available to expand the program? Are there enough health personnel trained to do the screenings in the special way that is sensitive to Chinese American women? When screenings identify cancer in many more women, are sufficient resources available to provide the needed follow-on treatment services? For these additional treatment services, are clinics able and willing to provide them, in view of other contextual factors they are facing (e.g., reduced health service payments, strained clinic support budgets)?

To summarize, CA is most intense and time consuming during the first stage of an evaluation, during planning. At a CA-focused meeting or series of meetings, the evaluator (and possibly other relevant stakeholders) identifies the most relevant context factors and considers their implications in planning the evaluation components and operations. As the evaluation progresses into the implementation stage, CA shifts to more of a monitoring process, where the evaluator checks decisions that were made earlier and identifies any adjustments that might be necessary. At the final evaluation stage, decision making and use, CA continues to involve monitoring but an important new type of focus is added, on the implications of recommendations and actions. Although CA becomes less intense in the second and third stages, we still recommend a CA-focused activity (e.g., a meeting specifically focused on CA) in order that the CA-related issues and implications can be identified and any needed actions can be taken.

Conclusion

As with many approaches and techniques in evaluation, there is a mix of benefits, limitations, and challenges involved in contextual assessment. We see three main benefits. First, CA gives the evaluator an opportunity to anchor and then reanchor the evaluation with explicit attention to different context issues. This reanchoring can be a way for the evaluator to capitalize on opportunities for a stronger evaluation. For example, in the case of the breast cancer screening program described above, the unexpected revelation by a well-known Chinese-American woman of her own breast cancer, identified through screening and then successfully treated, provides the opportunity to track sharp increases in the number of program screenings, likely due to this unexpected event in the broader environment. In this case, a context issue becomes much more than a confounding condition; it becomes a useful key to understanding what makes a program work. Second, context assessment makes conscious what evaluators sometimes only consider fleetingly or unconsciously. Evaluators typically have many pressures throughout the evaluation planning–implementation–use cycle, and, by moving context to the list of specific issues that an evaluator regularly checks, the chances are improved that significant context-related factors will be identified early and their implications incorporated into the evaluation process. Third, context assessment makes formal what is sometimes considered informally, thereby increasing the salience of context issues in the evaluation-related deliberations. In the schedule of tasks and deliverables for an evaluation, an evaluator who has adopted CA could list three time points in the evaluation activities when CA would be done and when a brief report of this would be produced or possibly presented orally for discussion with a key set of representative stakeholders. It would provide an opportunity for reconsideration of old issues and incorporation of new ones.

Context assessment also has its limitations and challenges. First, it is not a perfect process, with a comprehensive checklist to apply to all situations. Although we have identified five main areas to attend to, and given suggestions of dimensions and subdimensions within these areas to consider, context assessment cannot be rigidly defined and requires subjective judgments. Each evaluator brings his or her own perspectives, experiences, and background; these cannot be shed or set aside. Instead, these become lenses that can distort what the evaluator sees and understands. Sharing the results of a context assessment with the primary stakeholders for an intervention can help check or counter inherent evaluator biases. Second, CA does not guarantee that all relevant factors will be identified. Programs and contexts are complex and multifaceted, and, with the passage of time, these aspects can multiply. Third, context assessment requires some extra time and energy on the part of the evaluator and others, including program sponsors and funders, although these concerns need not become a major issue. The benefits of CA should more than compensate by identifying and incorporating important factors early, thereby making the evaluation even stronger, more comprehensive, and more useful.

If context matters, as Rog stated at the outset of her presidential address and in Chapter 2 of this issue (Rog, 2012), context assessment provides a way to recognize this and act on it. Although the importance of context has been noted by many working in the field, both in the United States and around the world, there has not been a systematic way to address it during the different stages of the evaluation process. We believe context assessment is a first step in making context more explicit and thereby increasing the likelihood that important contextual factors are in the mix of the primary evaluation considerations, particularly at the beginning stages of evaluation planning. We encourage evaluators to put our framework into use and then to assess the utility of the CA process critically. We believe our experiences and those of others, such as the authors in this volume, have demonstrated the utility of paying attention to context in an explicit way. The context framework and the CA process provide a way to do this systematically so that we can begin to deepen and share our knowledge of how contextual factors operate in all stages of evaluation. With more experience and greater knowledge, we will be better able to strengthen evaluation planning, implementation, and decision making/use, thereby increasing the chances that evaluation makes a difference.

References

Dahler-Larsen, J., & Schwandt, T. A. (2012). Political culture as context for evaluation. In D. J. Rog, J. L. Fitzpatrick, & R. F. Conner (Eds.), *Context: A framework for its influence on evaluation practice. New Directions for Evaluation, 135,* 75–87.

Fitzpatrick, J., Christie, C., & Mark, M. (2009). *Evaluation in action: Interviews with expert evaluators.* Thousand Oaks, CA: Sage.

LaFrance, J., Nichols, R., & Kirkhart, K. E. (2012). Culture writes the script: On the centrality of context in indigenous evaluation. In D. J. Rog, J. L. Fitzpatrick, & R. F. Conner (Eds.), *Context: A framework for its influence on evaluation practice. New Directions for Evaluation, 135,* 59–74.

Rog, D. J. (2009, November). *Toward context-sensitive evaluation practice.* Presidential Address. Evaluation 2009: 23rd annual conference of the American Evaluation Association, Orlando, FL.

Rog, D. J. (2012). When background becomes foreground: Toward context-sensitive evaluation practice. In D. J. Rog, J. L. Fitzpatrick, & R. F. Conner (Eds.), *Context: A framework for its influence on evaluation practice. New Directions for Evaluation, 135,* 25–40.

Thurston, L. P., Smith, C. A., Genskow, K., Prokopy, L. S., & Hargrove, W. L. (2012). The social context of water quality improvement evaluation. In D. J. Rog, J. L. Fitzpatrick, & R. F. Conner (Eds.), *Context: A framework for its influence on evaluation practice. New Directions for Evaluation, 135,* 41–58.

Ross F. Conner *is professor emeritus at the University of California–Irvine, in the School of Social Ecology, Department of Planning, Policy and Design, and is a past president of the American Evaluation Association and of the International Organization for Cooperation in Evaluation (IOCE).*

Jody L. Fitzpatrick *is associate professor in the School of Public Affairs at the University of Colorado–Denver and will be the president of the American Evaluation Association in 2013.*

Debra J. Rog *is an associate director at Westat and president of The Rockville Institute. She was the 2009 president of the American Evaluation Association.*

INDEX

A

Abma, T. A., 10
Accountability: core values of relational, 66; IEF involvement of community, 70–71
AEA Evaluation Policy Task Force, 8
African Evaluation Association, 19
AIR, 82
Alberti, M., 77, 78, 80
Alkin, M., 1, 26
Allison, B., 46
American Evaluation Association (AEA), 8, 14, 90
American evaluation models, 19–20
American Indian Higher Education Consortium, 60
American Indians. *See* Indian communities
American Journal of Evaluation, 1, 8
Arnold, M. E., 27

B

Bamberger, M., 18, 30
Basso, K. H., 62
Bennett, G., 83
Best management practices (BMPs), 43
Bhola, H. S., 18
Bickel, W. E., 32
Birnbaum, M., 29, 45
Born, S. M., 46
Braverman, M. T., 27, 32
Broader environment/setting context: evaluation area of, 28*fig,* 29–30; Great Lakes Regional Water Program (GLRWP) evaluation, 52–53; reviewing the process of, 92–93; watershed intervention evaluation of, 45–49. *See also* Environment evaluation
Brown, M., 44
Bruyninckx, H., 44

C

Cajete, G., 62
Ceiba (The Tree of Life), 64–65
Chen, H. T., 70
Cherokee basket story, 67
Chouinard, J. A., 9, 14, 16
Christie, C. A., 13, 27, 94
CIPP (context-input-process-product) evaluation model, 10
CIPP Evaluation Model Checklist, 10
Clean Water Act, 50, 52
Conner, R. F., 5, 6, 20, 89, 105
Constantine, N. A., 32
Context: considering some definitions of, 8–9; culturally contextualizing validity of, 70–72; culture as, 4, 9, 13–16; description of, 7–8, 27, 75–76; how evaluation is shaped by, 1, 5, 8, 25–32; new focus examining evaluation role of, 1–5; political culture as evaluation, 75–86; understanding the problematic notion of, 81–85; water quality evaluation, 43–49

Context areas: broader environment/setting, 28*fig,* 29–30, 52–53, 92–93; decision-making context, 28*fig,* 31–32, 37–38, 54–55, 90; evaluation context, 28*fig,* 29, 30–31, 53–54, 90; intervention context, 28*fig,* 29, 51–52, 91; the phenomenon and the problem, 27–29, 43–45, 50–51, 90; social-contextual denominators, 45–49
Context assessment (CA): applying to evaluation, 95–103; description of, 5; examining the process of, 89; function of using, 93; how evaluators can learn to use, 93–94
Context assessment (CA) process: step 1: context assessment for evaluation planning, 95–99; step 2: context for evaluation implementation, 99–101; step 3: context assessment for evaluation decision making and use, 101–103
Context in evaluation: CIPP (context-input-process-product) evaluation model, 10; cross-cultural approach to culture as context, 13–16; historical roots of, 9–13; international evaluations and, 16–20
Context-sensitive evaluation: actionable evidence during, 37–38; broader environment/setting, 28*fig,* 29–30, 52–53, 92–93; continued challenges of practicing, 38; decision-making context, 28*fig,* 31–32, 37–38, 54–55, 90; evaluation context, 28*fig,* 30–31; examining the practice of, 26–27; extending the framework of, 94–95; indigenous evaluation framework (IEF) as application of, 72–73, 92–93; involving stakeholders in process of, 32; nature of the intervention, 28*fig,* 29, 51–52, 91; nature of the phenomenon and problem in, 27–29, 43–45, 50–51, 90; reviewing the application process of, 90–93; strategies used for, 33–37. *See also* Evaluation
Context-sensitive strategies: for improving accuracy of estimates of program effects, 34–35; for improving the explanatory power of our studies, 35–37; to rule in or out alternative explanations, 33–34
Cousins, J. b., 9, 14, 16
Cram, F., 2, 15
Crazy Bull, C., 69
Cross-cultural evaluation: CRE (culturally responsive evaluation) approach to, 14–15; cultural competence required for, 15; culture as context in, 13–16
Cultural competence, 15
Culturally responsive evaluation (CRE) model, 14–15
Culture: context as defined by, 4, 9, 13–16; contexualizing validity through, 70–72; cross-cultural evaluation approach to context and, 13–16; Danish political culture (Version I), 76–79; Danish political culture (Version II), 79–81; indigenous evaluation framework (IEF) on centrality of context and, 59–60

78; the watershed approach to water quality in, 42–43; Wikipedia equality ranking of the, 77
Urban Institute, 82
U.S. Environmental Protection Agency (USEPA), 42, 49, 52–53
U.S. school cultural diversity, 15–16

V
Validity: culturally contexualizing, 70–72; justificatory perspective of multicultural, 71–72
VanDeveer, S. D., 49
Vedung, E., 78
Veenhoven, R., 77

W
Wallis, A., 20
Water pollutants: evaluating the watershed approach to address, 43–56; terminology used to describe, 43; the watershed approach to address, 42–43
Water quality: examining evaluation of, 43–56; terminology to describe impairment of, 43; the watershed approach to, 42–43
Water quality evaluation denominators: differential evaluation ethos, 48–49; identifying and measuring outcomes, 47–48; stakeholder diversity, 45–47
Water quality interventions evaluation: conclusions and recommendations for, 55–56; Great Lakes Regional Water Program (GLRWP), 49–55; reviewing the process of, 90–91

Watershed evaluation social indicators: broader environment setting context, 52–53; decision making context, 54–55; evaluation context, 53–54; intervention context, 51–52; phenomenon/problem context, 50–51; for water quality management and evaluation, 49–50
Watershed intervention: description of, 42; evaluation of, 43–56; social-contextual denominators of the, 45–49; water quality problems addressed using the, 42–43
Watershed interventions evaluation: problem context of, 43–45; setting context of the, 45–49; social indicators in, 49–55
Weber-Pillwax, C., 62, 64
Weiss, C. H., 1, 2, 8, 11, 12, 26, 27
Wernet, S., 33
WestSTAT, 82
Wholey, J. S., 2, 11, 12, 34
Wilson, S., 62, 66, 71
Winter Count story, 67–68
Witter, S., 46
Wolakokiciyapi (learning Lakota ways of life in community), 65
Wood, C., 41
Woope (Lakota laws), 71
World Bank, 82
Worthen, B.R., 17

Y
Yin, R. K., 35

ORDER FORM SUBSCRIPTION AND SINGLE ISSUES

DISCOUNTED BACK ISSUES:

Use this form to receive 20% off all back issues of *New Directions for Evaluation*.
All single issues priced at **$23.20** (normally $29.00)

TITLE	ISSUE NO.	ISBN
_____	_____	_____
_____	_____	_____
_____	_____	_____

Call 888-378-2537 or see mailing instructions below. When calling, mention the promotional code JBNND to receive your discount. For a complete list of issues, please visit www.josseybass.com/go/ev

SUBSCRIPTIONS: (1 YEAR, 4 ISSUES)

☐ New Order ☐ Renewal

U.S.	☐ Individual: $89	☐ Institutional: $295
CANADA/MEXICO	☐ Individual: $89	☐ Institutional: $335
ALL OTHERS	☐ Individual: $113	☐ Institutional: $369

Call 888-378-2537 or see mailing and pricing instructions below.
Online subscriptions are available at www.onlinelibrary.wiley.com

ORDER TOTALS:

Issue / Subscription Amount: $ _____

Shipping Amount: $ _____
(for single issues only – subscription prices include shipping)

Total Amount: $ _____

SHIPPING CHARGES:
First Item $6.00
Each Add'l Item $2.00

(No sales tax for U.S. subscriptions. Canadian residents, add GST for subscription orders. Individual rate subscriptions must be paid by personal check or credit card. Individual rate subscriptions may not be resold as library copies.)

BILLING & SHIPPING INFORMATION:

☐ **PAYMENT ENCLOSED:** *(U.S. check or money order only. All payments must be in U.S. dollars.)*

☐ **CREDIT CARD:** ☐ VISA ☐ MC ☐ AMEX

Card number _____ Exp. Date _____

Card Holder Name _____ Card Issue # _____

Signature _____ Day Phone _____

☐ **BILL ME:** *(U.S. institutional orders only. Purchase order required.)*

Purchase order # _____
Federal Tax ID 13559302 • GST 89102-8052

Name _____

Address _____

Phone _____ E-mail _____

Copy or detach page and send to: **John Wiley & Sons, One Montgomery Street, Suite 1200, San Francisco, CA 94104-4594**

Order Form can also be faxed to: **888-481-2665**

PROMO JBNND